INDIA-TAIWAN RELATIONS IN ASIA AND BEYOND

The Future

INDIA-TAIWAN RELATIONS IN ASIA AND BEYOND

The Future

Editor

Jagannath P. Panda

Foreword by

Jayant Prasad

Director General

Institute for Defence Studies and Analyses

idsa

INSTITUTE FOR DEFENCE STUDIES & ANALYSES

NEW DELHI

PENTAGON PRESS

India-Taiwan Relations in Asia and Beyond: The Future

Editor: Jagannath P. Panda

First Published in 2016

ISBN 978-81-8274-904-7

Published by

PENTAGON PRESS
206, Peacock Lane, Shahpur Jat,
New Delhi-110049
Phones: 011-64706243, 26491568
Telefax: 011-26490600
email: rajan@pentagonpress.in
website: www.pentagonpress.in

In association with
Institute for Defence Studies and Analyses
No. 1, Development Enclave,
New Delhi-110010
Phone: +91-11-26717983
Website: www.idsa.in

Printed at Aegean Offset Printers, Greater Noida

Contents

Foreword

It is a pleasure to join the commemorative volume marking the 20th anniversary of the establishment, in 1995, of the India-Taipei Association and the Taipei Economic and Cultural Center – the respective representative offices of India and Taiwan in Taipei and New Delhi. These offices immensely contribute to strengthening the friendship and cooperation between our two peoples.

A day-long conference organised in the Institute for Defence Studies and Analyses on the occasion focused on the future of this important relationship. This volume comprises papers presented at the conference, for which the Institute is grateful to the editor and all the contributors.

India remains invested in strengthening its relations with Taiwan, which go back to India's pre-independence days. Indians fondly recall the 1942 visit of Taiwan's great leader, Mr. Chiang Kai-Shek, who later became President of the Republic of China, and his support for India's freedom struggle. This steadily growing relationship has been grounded in a shared commitment to democracy, pluralism, and the rule of law, and increasingly, the common interests of the two economies.

Taiwan remains remarkably well-integrated with the international community, despite its constrained diplomatic space and the volatility of its relations with the People's Republic of China. The People's Republic of China, notwithstanding political tensions, has a strong and multi-faceted engagement with Taiwan. India could follow its example in deepening its economic ties with Taiwan, as many other major countries in Asia and beyond have done. It is an island of opportunities for commerce, investments, education, and scientific innovation, and provides an alternative window to Chinese language, culture, and civilisation. Taiwan, therefore, deserves India's greater attention for collaborative ventures and partnerships – a potential that has not yet been fully realised.

Both India and Taiwan have been responsible for the relative neglect of their mutual economic exchanges. Taiwan has not, so far, been a central element of India's 'Look East', and now 'Act East' policy, nor has Taiwan looked seriously to forging economic ties beyond Southeast Asia. Two way trade, which grew from $934 million in 1995 to a high point of $7.569 billion in 2011, showed an early plateauing trend. By the end of 2013, cumulative Taiwanese foreign direct investment (FDI) inflows in India of $1.4 billion, while three times more than China's investment in India, for the same period, of just under $500 million, is a very small fraction of Taiwan's overall foreign investment portfolio. Global FDI flows to India have, meanwhile, increased from $24 billion in 2012 to $44.2 billion in 2015.

The good news is that several big ticket investments from Taiwan are now on the anvil, straddling areas such as the real estate sector and communications, for projects that could entail investments of many multiples of the existing Taiwanese FDI in India. The 'Make in India' and 'Digital India' initiatives, in particular, offer opportunities for a marriage of Indian human resource and software skills, and Taiwanese technology and electronics. Both sides are also making a more determined effort to promote greater familiarity among their business and industry leaders and people-to-people contacts, which were deficient in the past. Even the strategic communities of India and Taiwan, involving their think-tanks and universities, are now freely interacting with each other.

Over the past two decades, the unofficial relations between India and Taiwan have grown into an interaction of significant potential. Taiwan can contribute to India's ongoing transformation, which has followed the progressive un-fettering of the Indian economy over the past quarter century. At a time when India is stepping up its focus on manufacturing and Taiwan is looking beyond China and Japan in promoting its 'Go South' policy, there is an excellent opportunity for both to deepen their engagement. High-technology trade and investment, and augmented educational and scientific exchange programmes, are areas that have perhaps the greatest promise for this. On the 20th anniversary of establishing their representative offices in Taipei and New Delhi, India and Taiwan appear poised for a more realistic and forward-looking relationship in the decade ahead.

Jayant Prasad
Director General
Institute for Defence Studies and Analyses

Special Note

This book is a collection of several papers presented at the one-day conference on "*Perspectives in India-Taiwan Relations in Asia and Beyond: The Future*" to commemorate the 20th anniversary of the establishment of the respective Representative Offices in India and in the Republic of China (Taiwan) in 1995. The conference, jointly organized by the Taipei Economic and Cultural Center in India (TECC) and the Institute for Defence Studies and Analyses (IDSA) on 8 December 2015, was mainly to retrospect the relations between India and Taiwan of the past 20 years and to explore ways to enhance the relations from diverse perspectives for the next 20 years. I am glad to see the papers being published today.

TECC was honoured to invite a well-known business leader and five outstanding scholars from Taiwan to participate in the conference. They are: **Mr. Theodore M. H. Huang (黃茂雄)**, Chairman of TECO Group; **Dr. Tuan Yao Cheng (鄭端耀)**, Professor and Dean of the College of Humanities and Information, University of Kang-Ning; **Dr. Francis Yi-hua Kan (甘逸驊)**, Associate Research Fellow, Institute of International Relations (IIR), National Cheng-Chi University; **Dr. Chun Lee (李淳)**, Deputy Executive Director of WTO and RTA Center, Chung-Hua Institution for Economic Research (CIER), Taipei; **Ms. Kristy Tsun-Tzu Hsu (徐遵慈)**, Programme Director at the Taiwan ASEAN Studies Center (TASC) and Associate Research Fellow at the Taiwan WTO and RTA Center, Chung Hua Institution for Economic Research (CIER); and **Dr. Fu-Kuo Liu (劉復國)**, Research Fellow, Institute of International Relations (IIR), National Cheng-Chi University. They, along with senior Indian Ambassadors and top international relations experts, conducted a comprehensive and in-depth discussion on several important topics, including the Ma-Xi meeting, TPP, RCEP and regional integration, Indo-Pacific peace and prosperity, etc.

I would like to express my deepest appreciation to Shri (Amb.) Jayant Prasad, Director General of IDSA and his capable colleagues for their professional support and participation in organising the conference, as well as for facilitating the publication of the papers. I would also like to thank all the paper presenters and chairpersons of the sessions for their hard work during the conference.

This publication marks a milestone of India-Taiwan relations over the past 20 years. It would be useful to the academic and diplomatic circles interested in further understanding the diverse aspects of the unique India-Taiwan bilateral relations. Looking ahead, our two countries are amidst a sea of potential and possibilities. The scope for collaboration cannot be limited to upgrade trade and business relations but should also further deepen bilateral cooperation in the areas of culture, education and human resources, etc. between our peoples. I believe that there is a huge room to expand and further develop these mutual beneficial exchanges and cooperation. Looking beyond, let us work together to improve upon the cordial India-Taiwan relationship for the next 20 years.

New Delhi
May 2016

H.E. Chung-Kwang Tien
Representative
Taipei Economic and Cultural Center in India

Acknowledgements

This volume is an outcome of the conference that the Institute for Defence Studies and Analyses (IDSA) in collaboration with the Taipei Economic and Cultural Center (TECC) held in New Delhi on 8 December 2015 at IDSA. The conference was organised to commemorate the 20th anniversary of the establishment of their respective Representative Offices in Taipei and New Delhi by India and Taiwan. I am thankful to both IDSA and TECC for extending their support and assistance in conducting the conference and in bringing out this volume.

As the conference coordinator and editor of this volume, I owe much gratitude to a few dignitaries and esteemed persons. I am thankful to Shri Jayant Prasad, Director General of IDSA, for extending all-out support for the conference and taking a serious interest in it. I am also thankful to Brig. (Retd.) Rumel Dahiya for his guidance and suggestions for the conduct of the event. H.E. Chung-Kwang Tien, Representative of TECC in New Delhi, was generous in extending support and encouragement for the event and, most importantly, inviting a set of outstanding Taiwanese experts from Taiwan. A special note of thanks goes to Mr. Theodore Huang, Chairman of the TECO Group and Honorary Chairman of the Chinese National Association of Industry and Commerce (CNIAC), for gracing the occasion. Mr. Pradeep Kumar Rawat, Joint Secretary (East Asia) of the Ministry of External Affairs (MEA) of the Government of India, honoured the occasion with his keynote speech.

In the course of this conference and editing this volume, I have accumulated many debts. I am thankful to Prof. Alka Acharya of the

Institute of Chinese Studies (ICS) in New Delhi, Prof. B.R. Deepak and Prof. Srikanth Kondapalli of the Jawaharlal Nehru University (JNU), Prof. P. Stobdan of IDSA, Mr. Manoj Joshi of the Observer Research Foundation (ORF) in New Delhi, Prof. Sreemati Chakrabarti of Delhi University, Amb. R. Rajgopalan, Prof. Cheng Tuan Yao of the University of Kang-Ning, and Prof. Lee Chun of the WTO and RTC Center of Taipei. They amplified the conference by chairing the sessions and participating in the panel discussions. I am also thankful to (Late) Isabel Lo, Mr. Oliver Harn and Col. Jung Kee-Chyuan for their timely cooperation and assistance in the conduct of the conference and in bringing out this volume.I appreciate and offer my thanks to my colleagues in the East Asia Centre in IDSA for their cooperation in conducting the conference.

The contributors to this volume have been the linchpin behind the success of the conference and in enabling the production of this volume. Their scholarship enriched the conference. These set of experts and scholars are undoubtedly the backbone of India-Taiwan relations.

Dr. Jagannath P. Panda

List of Contributors

Dr. Jagannath P. Panda is Research Fellow and Centre Coordinator for East Asia at the Institute for Defence Studies and Analyses (IDSA), New Delhi.

Dr. Francis Yi-hua Kan is a Fellow at the Institute of International Relations (IIR), National Chengchi University, Taiwan.

Dr. Prashant Kumar Singh is Associate Fellow at the Institute for Defence Studies and Analyses (IDSA), New Delhi.

Dr. Jabin T. Jacob is Assistant Director and Fellow at the Institute of Chinese Studies (ICS), New Delhi.

Dr. Ritu Agarwal is Associate Professor at the School of International Studies (SIS), Jawaharlal Nehru University, New Delhi.

Ms. Kristy Tsun-Tzu Hsu is the Director of Taiwan-ASEAN study centre, Chung Hua Institution for Economic Research (CIER), Taiwan.

Dr. Suresh T. Gopalan is Associate Professor at the School of Social Science, Jawaharlal Nehru University, New Delhi.

Dr. Arvind B. Yelery is Associate Fellow at the Institute of Chinese Studies, New Delhi.

Dr. Fu-Kuo Liu is a Fellow at the Institute of International Relations (IIR), National Chengchi University, Taiwan.

Dr. Cherian Samuel is Associate Fellow at the Institute for Defence Studies and Analyses (IDSA), New Delhi.

1

Introduction

Jagannath P. Panda

India-Taiwan relations are a lesser studied subject in the international relations academic discipline. Given the strategic importance both India and Taiwan hold in Asia, the academic and scholarly pursuit has not really matched to discuss and punctuate the importance of this relationship in the bilateral, regional and global contexts. Literature is fast appearing on the subject, which mostly concentrates on the scope and potential of India-Taiwan bilateral relations. Most of it expresses optimism that there are many opportunities for the two countries to cooperate. But it falls short in evaluating the relationship from a comprehensive perspective, taking the contemporary evolving realities into account, which will matter for the future of India-Taiwan relations. This volume is a progressive addition to the newly arrived literature on the subject and covers a wider spectrum of India-Taiwan relations in the bilateral and regional contexts and beyond. It highlights the bilateral and regional contours of these relations and promotes a possible strategic deliberation that the importance of these relations may not necessarily be confined to the bilateral context. It contextualises the vitality of Asia and beyond in India-Taiwan relations and deliberates on the potential areas of strength where they can possibly cooperate in the future.

Over the last two decades, India-Taiwan relations have progressed considerably despite not having diplomatic status to their ties. Their trade and economic contacts have improved. Taiwanese investments have been promoted in India and educational linkages have also expanded between the two. Although because of the constraints of one-China policy the two sides do not have diplomatic ties, their bilateral working relations have always generated a political context. Political leaders from both sides have intermittently visited each other. This exchange of visits, growth in trade and economic contacts and expanding educational contacts point to the upward trend in their engagement.

The key behind this progressive upward trend has been the establishment of representative offices by both sides in each other's capitals. The India-Taipei Association (ITA) in Taiwan and the Taipei Economic and Cultural Center (TECC) in India were established in 1995, which have functioned to give a direction to the relations between the two countries. They have worked more as official channels without any formal diplomatic attachments. Their nomenclature – 'association' and 'economic and cultural center' – explains this narrative. They have been the official channels of communication to promote the working relations between India and Taiwan on every front – politics to economics, society to culture and think-tanks and universities to civil society interactions.

Today, on the occasion of the commemoration of 20 years of the establishment of the representative offices, one needs to inquire about the future potential and scope of India-Taiwan relations and to what extent the two sides can upgrade their ties further. Three possible conditions that could bring India and Taiwan together in the current and future contexts are: *first*, the current foreign policy course of the two sides is conducive towards a growing relationship between them, which can create better conditions for their cooperation; *second*, the regional economic conditions and integration process allow them to think about a regional mode of contacts today, which was not the case earlier; and *third*, the scope and interest to expand the bilateral contacts without really affecting their relations with the People's Republic of China (PRC).

To begin with, the current foreign policy directions of both India and Taiwan open an optimistic scenario for their future relations. A consonance exists in India's Act East policy and Taiwan's Go South policy. Go South has pursued a pragmatic approach of establishing representative offices in South-East Asia. Its main intent has been to solidify Taiwan's economic contacts with the countries of the region. Taiwan factors India prominently in its Go South policy. The margin to expand the scope of political contacts may remain low due to the one-China policy, but further economic contacts can create opportunities for better political contacts between the two sides at bilateral as well as regional levels. The newly elected Democratic Progressive Party (DPP) presidential candidate Tsai Ing-wen has long advocated that India is an important factor in Taiwan's Go South policy and the DPP would like to promote Taiwan's 'new southward policy'.[1] This policy is intended to promote Taiwan's economic engagement with countries other than China.[2] India must appreciate this policy direction and identify the consonance factors that will establish synergy between India's Act East and Taiwan's Go South policies. Act East aims to enhance India's engagement with East Asia and the broader Asia-Pacific region. Taiwan can be ranked high in this policy, factoring in as a special economic region for India's overseas economic interests. Besides, Go South will aptly support the Indian government's Make in India campaign, where a lot of Taiwanese investment can flow into India. This synergy between Taiwan and India needs to be established in the foreign policy stratagem.

India and Taiwan must also capitalise on the evolving regional architecture, which offers them new opportunities not only to cooperate but also to enhance their respective regional positions. The regional order is in a flux, where a power transition is taking place amidst a range of economic and strategic competitions. The focus of the ensuing regional order may be on Asia-Pacific, but the construct of Asia-Pacific is gradually being transformed into Indo-Pacific. In this transitional order, countries and their respective policies thrust intently on maritime security, regional economic integration and free-trading economic collaborating models. In these three areas India and Taiwan currently have minimal cooperation though the ideas are unfolding at experts' and scholarly levels that the two sides can start deliberating on a set of engagements which can be strategic yet non-political.[3] Non-traditional security cooperation in maritime areas is one such area. Both India and Taiwan also need greater regional integration through participating in multilateral forums in which both require each other's support and backing. Similarly, against the backdrop of the ongoing trade liberalising economic models like the Regional Comprehensive Economic Partnership (RCEP), the Trans-Pacific Partnership (TPP) and the Free Trade Area of Asia-Pacific (FTAAP), India and Taiwan would need each other in terms of generating support for their participation and, importantly, in the negotiation process.

Regional cooperation between India and Taiwan is still conjectural in nature. Therefore what is important in their relations is the prospect of their bilateral contacts. Even though since the establishment of their representative offices in 1995, India-Taiwan bilateral contacts have progressed to some extent, the potential of this cooperation has not really thrived and has been restricted because of the one-China policy. The obvious query is: how will India and Taiwan approach their future bilateral ties amidst the Chinese obsession over Taiwan's sovereignty issue? Much will depend upon how their governments approach each other in terms of expanding their bilateral ties. It is unlikely that the incoming DPP dispensation will pursue an anti-China foreign policy. But that will not impede it from pursuing a policy that will promote Taiwan's interest beyond the Chinese prism. New Delhi on its part will neither renounce its traditional one-China policy nor interact with Taiwan in a way that will affect its relations with the PRC. What needs to be seen is whether India will enhance its non-diplomatic relations with Taiwan, primarily in areas like economic and cultural engagement. The onus remains on capitalising on the bilateral relations and identifying the specific areas of cooperation.

This volume, which arises from an open spectrum of experts' views and opinions, identifies some of these areas of cooperation. Most of these views may seem gratuitous. Yet, one needs to acknowledge that India-Taiwan relations need a measure of conviction and ambition that will push their relations further both at the bilateral and regional levels. True, progress in India-Taiwan relations is heavily dependent on bilateral contacts, yet the regional context and conditions equally matter. Francis Yi-hua Kan in his paper argues that given the context of Taiwan Strait where mainland China-Taiwan relations and US-China dynamics are always on the threshold, both India and Taiwan must capitalise on the fact to build a regional dimension to their relationship. Both can be facilitators of a 'healthy' regional and global order. The author also sees the merit of India-Taiwan cooperation in areas like democracy promotion and high-tech cooperation which can solidify the two sides' relations further. Ritu Agarwal also identifies 'democracy' as a strength in India's and Taiwan's context. Building a context between the 'two democracies' and 'two governing systems', she argues that there is scope for India to learn from Taiwan's democratic system and its practice. Taiwan also must take India's democratic experience as a respected lesson to find synergy both between the two sides and to solidify its own governance system.

Trade and economic cooperation is one area which can be the real basis of India-Taiwan relations. The intent should not only be aimed at maximising the trade contacts between the two sides, which is around US$6 billion currently, but equally to establish a comprehensive economic partnership that will sustain their overall relations. Educational exchanges, cultural cooperation and science & technology collaboration are potential areas that can be the basis of this cooperation. Cherian Samuel's paper explores how India and Taiwan can cooperate in a potential area like cyber security. The author argues that as titans of hardware and software, Taiwan and India respectively must see cyberspace as one of the potential areas for cooperation. There is a lack of direction between India and Taiwan on how to cooperate in the cyber security area even though both countries are victims of cyber security threats.

There is also a greater regional context to India-Taiwan cooperation. Regional economic cooperation is one such area that can be explored. Kristy Hsu in her paper sees the India-Taiwan economic partnership in the greater Asian context and argues that Taiwan has the potential to emerge as India's 'strategic economic' partner. She further argues that India has to also rise to factor Taiwan in a changing Asia and contribute to Taiwan's global value chain networks. She also sees India-Taiwan economic cooperation in the context of rebalancing Taiwan's economic relations with mainland China.

Prashant Kumar Singh's chapter offers an Indian perspective on India-Taiwan relations and identifying the potential areas for India to build a cooperative relation with Taiwan. Positioning Taiwan in India's current Act East policy more deliberately, the author argues that India's approach towards Taiwan is not entirely restricted within the prism of the one-China policy; rather, India can enhance its Taiwan reach within the broader spectrum of its one-China policy – that Taiwan is a Chinese province yet an exclusive cooperation between the two sides is permissible. Jabin T. Jacob endorses such a perspective and argues that Taiwan must factor more intently in India's Act East policy if New Delhi intends to see its engagement with East Asia purposive. The author further argues that there are many opportunities in India-Taiwan relations, but the problem in these relations is the lack of ambition and creativity to nurture them further.

Suresh T. Gopalan sees the emergence of a new context in India-Taiwan relations. In the author's view, the two sides may have distinctive historical routes but there was always a sense of consonance between them. The recent mutual discovery of both India and Taiwan as a palatable factor in each other's rising sphere is an interesting and welcome development. Besides, one of the highlights of the arguments in this book are the views on India-Taiwan relations in an Indo-Pacific construct. Jagannath P. Panda in his paper foresees that India and Taiwan need to tap the growing potential areas in the Indo-Pacific region to cooperate. The author argues that even though India and Taiwan do not have formal diplomatic ties, diplomacy has many nuances and gradations, which India and Taiwan can exploit to enhance their relations in an evolving Indo-Pacific order. Taiwan has to carefully prepare a path for itself in the regional order to seek India's support, whereas India has also equally to take an interest to cooperate with Taiwan in regional mechanisms and institutions. Both need to think ambitiously, not ambiguously, to enhance their regional cooperation.

Arvind Yelery argues that the economic integration process is one of the challenging aspects in regional politics currently, which India and Taiwan should not overlook. The author argues that China is undoubtedly an influential actor in the regional economic integration process but a synergy of cooperation and tapping the emerging potentials may emerge among India, China and Taiwan. India must take note that the Chinese are taking an interest in infrastructural development projects whereas Taiwanese companies are thrusting on innovation-led technologies and soft skills projects. Fu-Kuo Liu's chapter foresees a maritime strategic perspective in India-Taiwan relations in the context of Indo-Pacific. The author argues that both India and Taiwan must comprehend the importance of Indo-

Pacific in their relationship from a 'non-political' prism and should develop a new ground of common interest. He carefully builds a perspective to argue that India and Taiwan can cooperate in the maritime domain.

This book builds many perspectives on India-Taiwan relations. Most of these perspectives are essentially longstanding and conditioned by their relations which do not have a diplomatic status. What is new in this book is that there are new contexts emerging in India-Taiwan relations and which need to be capitalised on in bilateral, regional and global contexts. The issues may be established, but the conditions are new and emerging. The book not only puts India-Taiwan relations in a new milieu but also generates an improved regional standing for both sides that is a key to the regional order and condition. The relevance of this book is therefore projected to be timely and enduring.

NOTES

1. 'Taiwan has long followed "go south" policy: ministry', *Taipei Times,* 5 October 2015, http://www.taipeitimes.com/News/taiwan/archives/2015/10/05/2003629318 (accessed on 10 May 2016).
2. Matthew Strong, 'Tsai unveils Go South policy', *Taiwan News,* 22 September 2015, http://www.taiwannews.com.tw/etn/news_content.php?id=2808338 (accessed on 10 May 2016); see also Goh Sui Noi, 'Taiwan looks beyond China for growth', *Strait Times,* 16 October 2015, http://www.straitstimes.com/opinion/taiwan-looks-beyond-china-for-growth (accessed on 10 May 2016).
3. Jonathan Chin, 'Taiwan, India advised to counter Chinese expansion', *Taipei Times,* 23 January 2016, http://www.taipeitimes.com/News/taiwan/archives/2016/01/23/2003637871 (accessed on 10 May 2016).

2

The Ma-Xi Summit and Cross-Taiwan Strait Relations: Implications for Taiwan-India Cooperation

Francis Yi-hua Kan

The ground-breaking summit between the leaders of Taiwan and mainland China, held in Singapore on 7 November 2015, was a remarkable development in cross-strait history as well as East Asian security. It was the first such meeting since 1949, when the two sides across the Taiwan Strait split as a result of the end of the civil war. President Ma Ying-jeou and President Xi Jinping met at a time when the chronic tension between the two sides has considerably eased owing to Ma's rapprochement policy towards the mainland in the past seven and a half years. At the same time, the future of cross-strait relations could be volatile, depending upon whether the peace process will be kept on track after 2016. Stability and peace in the Taiwan Strait is an extraordinary case of conflict resolution and peace building in East Asia, where domestic and international strife has constantly looked imminent and the maritime powers are contending with territorial water disputes. In addition to its significance for Taiwan Strait security, the meeting between the two leaders also presents an outstanding model for the resolution of other international conflicts.

The cross-strait amelioration is unique in that it has been a bottom-up process of revolutionising ties, gradually and steadily. Many international conflicts elsewhere have been handled with a top-down approach, starting with high-level summits and grandiose agreements in times of escalating hostility, in the hope that they could result in workable relations and people-to-people interactions. Actually, they often lead nowhere.

Taiwan-mainland relations began with Taiwanese investors pouring resources and technologies into the mainland over the past thirty years; 8 million people visiting the other side this year; 40,000 students studying across the strait; a hundred flights crossing the borders weekly; 23 agreements aiming at improving people's well-being signed; and more than $170 billion bilateral annual trade. Semi-official talks over issues of direct interests of people started more than 20 years ago, followed by lower-rank officials' dialogues, and then ministerial-level meetings. The improvement of Taiwan-mainland relations has undergone a long process of tension reducing, confidence building, and peace-making. The cross-strait summit is a natural outcome.

After the level of negotiations between Taipei and Beijing has been upgraded to the top, the base of cooperation would be wider (direct contacts between more ministries) and deeper. Also, the summit meeting may stimulate governmental bureaucracies in charge of cross-strait policy to be more creative in cooperation with the other side. There maybe no treaties signed, no pretentious ceremonies held, and no joint statement issued, but more importance will be attached and more implications will be explored as a result of this landmark summit.

The Leaders' Incentives

Relations between the two sides had long been strained due to ideological and political divergences, keeping their ties on knife edge before 2008. Since his inauguration, President Ma over a relatively short period of time has proactively been committed to transforming the war-prone strait into peaceful waters. The news release of the Ma-Xi meeting came as a surprise and even consternation, with some analysts arguing that the meeting was a 'gamble'.[1]

Xi's Possible Audience

Domestic audience: The meeting posed a chance for Xi to show the domestic audience his confidence as a strong leader in dealing with external relations, including Taiwan. One way used by Xi to reinforce his image of strong leadership is to be assertive and forceful in foreign policy, such as China's intransigent stance over the South China Sea. Yet, President Xi took risks of initiating the cross-strait talk without aiming at any concrete 'political' compromise that had long been demanded by the mainland side. The ability of flexibility reinforces, rather than weaken, his image.

Taiwan's future leadership: As Dean Cheng, a China specialist of the Heritage Foundation indicates, Beijing would do whatever it could to forestall any sea-change in cross-strait relations caused by Taiwan's election results. While taking into account the foreseeable outcomes of Taiwan's presidential and parliamentary elections, President Xi may have intended to set a high bar for Taiwan's future leader, to be elected only a few months after the summit. He must also have realised the necessity of institutionalising the two-way communication mechanism and process which could facilitate future high-level dialogues with his Taiwanese counterparts, who may find it hard to reverse the trend. It would look problematic if Ma's successor is not able to create opportunities to meet their Chinese counterpart.

Taiwan people: The mainland side may have also tried to impress Taiwan's general public with Xi's charm offensive by initiating this summit meeting, argues Jerome A. Cohen, professor at School of Law, New York University.[2] China's soft image is a well-designed strategy to assuage the concerns of China's neighbours and beyond about its increasing capabilities and compelling ambition. An olive branch extended by President Xi in the run-up to Taiwan's general elections might neutralise the 'China factor' in the electorate's deliberations. Alternatively, President Xi may have hoped that a summit meeting of this kind might boost the ruling KMT government's popularity that has plummeted to an all-time low.

President Ma: As a typical example of Chinese-style strong leadership, President Xi maintains the formula of 'repayment for grace; grudges against revenge'. President Xi may have simply given credit to President Ma in recognition of his contributions to cross-strait stability. He therefore presented Ma an unprecedented amount of respect and dignity.

Ma's Possible Audience

History: The cross-strait reconciliation has been President Ma's flagship political achievement. An unexampled meeting between the heads of the formal rivals would enhance his image of a peace icon and solidify his legacy. Ralph Cossa, President of the Pacific Forum at the Center for Strategic and International Studies (CSIS), believes that this was Ma's primary objective and he achieved it. In retrospect, President Ma's contribution to a calm and peaceful cross-strait relationship has largely been ignored or demonised, particularly by the domestic audience. His mainland policy has strengthened – not undercut – Taiwan's security and strategic interests. Cossa maintains that Ma has not been given enough credit.[3] History will look favourably on him for being the first democratically elected Taiwan president to meet his counterpart from China.

Opposition party: A high-profile meeting between the Taiwanese and mainland leaders would exert great pressure on the Democratic Progressive Party (DPP) and its leader in making and adapting the party's China policy. The summit has helped President Ma assure his people that the course of wisdom is to continue cooperation with the mainland. The DPP Chairwoman, Tsai Ing-wen, considered *a presidential hopeful* for the 2016 election, may have to acknowledge the value of the 1992 consensus and the benefits of the cross-strait peace, and to preserve them accordingly.

The KMT: Domestic and international media widely speculated that President Ma might attempt to drum up voters' support desperately needed by his party. But Andrew J. Nathan, professor of political science, Columbia University, disagrees that Ma attended the summit with the expectation of altering the outcome of the upcoming elections.[4] Instead, he may contemplate that a special role as a peacemaker in cross-strait relations could be bestowed upon him after his retirement from government.

The Leaders' Appeals

The two leaders seized the opportunity of the world's media focus on the summit to send the message that they intended to deliver. They voiced their respective convictions as well as concerns publicly or behind the scene.

Xi's Appeals

Ethnic solidarity and national unity: President Xi attempted to communicate with the Taiwan people with the aim of winning hearts and minds by emphasising that, despite the cross-strait divide in the past several decades, the peoples across the strait belong to one big family. He believed that the reconciliation and cooperation committed by both sides in the past seven years reinforced the bonds. He continued that the dream of a Chinese rejuvenation crucially depends upon the end of the political separation that would restore China's pride.

Taiwan's future government: Xi was also raising the red flag that a critical crossroads was ahead for the next administration of Taiwan to take. One is a path of peaceful development, which has been taken in the last several years. To continue on this path, Taiwan should unswervingly oppose its independence and adhere to the 1992 consensus, the pivot of cross-strait reconciliation. The alternative is full of confrontation, separation and zero-sum-game hostility, leading Taiwan to lose in its course of peaceful development.

Taiwan independence: If Tsai's party wins in Taiwan's presidential and parliamentary elections, there is the challenge of her independence-leaning policy. The Taiwanese, particularly the younger generation, are increasingly attached to Taiwan's distinct identity separate from China's. Xi sent a blunt message to Taiwan that the most serious threat to cross-strait peaceful development is the Taiwan independence force and the separatist movements, which he accused of provoking cross-strait hostility and confrontation, jeopardising peace and stability.

Ma's Appeals

Don't rock the boat: The Ma administration designated the goals of the summit meeting as being in pursuit of 'consolidation of the 1992 consensus and maintenance of cross-strait peace'. Cross-strait stability and peace is a remarkable achievement, widely recognised by the international community. Ma would be averse to any reversal of course against this legacy of his.

Be patient: Future dialogue between the two sides should follow the step-by-step approach that has proved useful and practical. Any haste to touch upon political sensitivities, if chased after by the Chinese side, will do no good for cross-strait rapprochement.

Mainland's threats: The mainland continues to overlook the aspiration of the Taiwanese people for international space and national security. The latter resent China's stubborn efforts to marginalise Taiwan internationally. Also, China has continued to pose a serious threat to Taiwan's security with its advanced missiles and other military deployments.

Regional integration: The countries around Taiwan have strenuously cooperated in constructing various forms of regional integration, but Taiwan has been excluded from them mainly because of China's objection. President Ma has stressed that Taiwan's participation will be in the interests of all.

Both Symbolism and Substantiality

The Ma-Xi meeting was viewed by many as merely symbolic. But symbols can indeed create substance.[5] The summit has genuinely proven both its symbolic and substantial significance.

Symbolism

Equality and reciprocity: The fact that the two leaders, from once belligerent parties, now can shake hands and sit across the negotiating table is a phenomenal achievement. The meeting taking place in a third-party venue also indicates that it was not a low-key event, even from the mainland's perspective. It actually created an occasion of 'mutual non-subordination' between the two sides, something Beijing had long seen as a dangerous precedent and had fervently avoided.

Mutual non-denial: The meeting represented an indication, though indirect, of 'mutual non-denial' or even *de facto* 'mutual recognition' elaborated by

President Ma. The principles of Taiwan's dignity and equality between them have conspicuously been observed.

Taiwan's international standing: On the whole, the international community has assessed the Ma-Xi meeting positively. President Ma has been widely praised for his contribution to converting the sour cross-strait relations into amicable ties and to enhancing regional stability. For instance, the US has publicly acknowledged the success of the meeting and supported Taiwan by announcing a new package of arms sales to Taipei a fortnight after the meeting.

Confidence building: Sitting across the table with President Xi Jinping, President Ma earnestly expressed the concern of his people about the mainland's chronic threat to the island's security. He suggested that a hotline between the two sides should be installed to avoid any miscalculation. Gestures like this could lay a solid groundwork for mutual trust building.

Substantiality

Institutionalisation and normalisation: The bilateral relations have become more systematised. The meeting gives rise to the hope that summits would be routinised.[6]

Set a positive tone: The two leaders confirmed the common ground on which bilateral negotiations have been conducted and some mutual trust has been built. It is especially meaningful for Taiwan since dialogue and negotiations may become common in cross-strait interaction.

Gradual and steady approach: The agreement to set up a hotline between the agencies in charge of the bilateral relations is a sound example of the accumulation of small steps towards bigger projects.

What Should Be Done

The sustainability of the cross-strait rapprochement will depend on how serious Taiwan's next administration would be to adapt itself to the 1992 consensus and how flexible the mainland would be to respond. Both sides have to stick to the common ground on which they have strenuously built in the past several years and come up with possible alternatives acceptable to both. A serious standoff would kill the momentum of improvement.

On the Mainland Side

Taiwan's international space: China needs to answer Taiwan's aspirations for wider international participation, including regional cooperation like Regional Comprehensive Economic Partnership (RCEP) and Trans-Pacific Partnership (TPP). President Ma's call for Taiwan's better access to the international community was met by President Xi's partial agreement on a case-by-case basis and under appropriate titles, such as membership of the Asian Infrastructure Investment Bank (AIIB) and participation in China's One Belt, One Road (OBOR) initiative. The mainland should do much more to convince the Taiwanese people of its sincerity of taking care of their well-being, which can be enhanced by Taiwan's wider international participation.

Military threat: Mainland China should also seriously contemplate how to eliminate its military threat to Taiwan in terms of dispute solving between the two sides. Some American military experts, e.g. Richard Fisher of the International Assessment and Strategic Center, suggest that China should consider making some moves for genuine confidence building, including demilitarising the Nanjing Military Region, which currently is improving amphibious assault capabilities targeting Taiwan.

Seize the momentum: The Singapore meeting was a good start. To keep up the momentum, the mainland has to create a friendly environment and lift the barriers for future bilateral summits with whoever will be Taiwan's next president. Overall, the mainland has to take a concrete approach to convince the Taiwanese people that their demands for dignity, respect, sincerity and goodwill have been observed.

On the Taiwan Side

Informing the general public: The Taiwanese administrations have to double their efforts in informing the general public of the reality of a rising China with which Taiwan has to work and in convincing the people, particularly the young generations, of the necessity and importance of improving relations with the mainland.

The 1992 consensus: Whoever succeeds President Ma should value the cross-strait achievements hard earned by him. The 1992 consensus has laid a solid foundation for resumption of peace negotiation and constituted a framework where interactions and cooperation are conducted. The future president should respect and adhere to this consensus.

To understand the mainland better: With shared historical and cultural heritage and geographic proximity, Taiwan is advantageously placed to understand the Chinese politics, ideology, society, and mindset. It would be in Taiwan's interest to be most familiar with the mainland, particularly at this time of China's rapid rise to be a world-class power.

India-Taiwan Cooperation

The Taiwan Strait may now appear relatively calm, but this region has been the centre of gravity for the world economy and also the focus of the world's instability. It is also an area on which the cooperation and conflict between the US and China would have great impact. Taiwan and India should reach out to each other to extend their benevolent influence in promoting cooperation and preventing conflict among major powers and smaller players alike.

Partnership of civilian powers: In contrast to the concept of a military power, a civilian power centres on the normative dimension of the country's role as a substantial contributor to others, devoted to disaster relief, humanitarian assistance and development aid. It should focus on the promotion of democracy, human rights, rule of law, human dignity, civil liberty, as well as participation in post-conflict peacekeeping and stability promotion efforts. These are values shared by both Taiwan and India, who might form a partnership of civilian powers which could invite more like-minded countries to join. Taiwan and India could work together to promote a civilian, not military, global order.

Economic partners: Taiwan and India are trading powers too. India's current economic performance is distinctly impressive. It is experiencing an economic growth that China has enjoyed in the past two or three decades. At the PPP rate, India is already the world's third-largest economy worth $2 trillion and it might become number one by the mid-century. It will also enjoy a long-term demographic dividend, with 11 million extra people every year over the next 40 years, making India a youthful country. There will be 10 million additional jobs to be created, mostly non-agricultural work. This vast nation needs some reliable partners like Taiwan whose

SMEs (small and medium enterprises) and 'hidden champions' could contribute to India's continuing growth and ecological sustainability.

Hi-tech Cooperation: Both Taiwan and India possess the best strategic leverage for lasting success, i.e. human capital. Both countries also target hi-tech industries as the core of economic transformation. Today India is 'playing leapfrog',[7] facilitated by its Make in India initiative, which not only champions manufacturing industries but also stimulates hi-tech industries like renewable energy (e.g. Suzlon, the world's fifth-largest wind turbine manufacturer), healthcare industry (a target for eradicating tuberculosis and measles and immunising 90 per cent of children against a host of diseases; set up the world's biggest biometric database, 1 billion people, called Aadhaar), science and technology (in cities like Bengaluru and Hyderabad and brands like Infosys and Wipro), digital start-ups (more than 3,100 tech start-ups in 2014 alone), and e-commerce markets. Moreover, the Modi government plans to build 100 'smart cities' by 2020, generating millions of jobs. Taiwan has more than 30 years experience in making it a shining brand of innovation. Furthering cooperation in science and hi-tech industries between Taiwan and India will be highly complementary and reciprocal.

Facilitators of a 'healthy' regional and global order in the making: Confronting the continuing rise of China, both Taiwan and India, in being this great power's neighbours, share strategic interests. Taiwan has inherited the essence of Chinese cultural heritage. India is China's most populous and democratic bordering country. Both are well placed to influence the direction of China's rise and hence the region's stability. While Beijing promotes a 'Chinese way' for other developing countries to follow, the world's largest democracy could raise high the flag of an 'Indian way' with its free press, an independent judiciary, rapidly rising economy, and innovative entrepreneurship.[8] Prime Minister Narendra Modi proposes that it will be clear that this is 'India's century' by 2022 when the country celebrates its 75th anniversary of independence. Our two democracies share common interests in influencing the emerging regional and global order where a healthy US-China great-power relationship can enhance peace and where we can all thrive.

NOTES

1. For instance, 'Hands across the water', *The Economist*, 7 November 2015, http://www.economist.com/news/asia/21677559-leaders-china-and-taiwan-are-meet-first-time-their-history-hands-across.
2. 'Cross-Strait Summit: a win for Taiwan's President?' *Foreign Policy*, 8 November 2015, http://foreignpolicy.com/2015/11/08/cross-strait-summit-a-win-for-taiwans-president.
3. Quoted from 'Analysis: was Ma-Xi meeting a historic summit or farewell dinner?' *Defense News*, 15 November 2015, http://www.defensenews.com/story/defense/international/asia-pacific/2015/11/13/analysis-ma-xi-meeting-historic-summit-farewell-dinner/75694816.
4. 'Cross-Strait Summit: a win for Taiwan's President?' *Foreign Policy*, n. 2.
5. Richard C. Bush III, 'What the historic Ma-Xi meeting could mean for cross-strait relations', Brookings Institution, 9 November 2015, http://www.brookings.edu/blogs/order-from-chaos/posts/2015/11/09-ma-xi-meeting-singapore-bush.
6. 'Xi-Ma Summit has changed the status quo', *Asia Times*, 9 November 2015, http://atimes.com/2015/11/xi-ma-summit-has-changed-the-status-quo.
7. 'Government and technology: playing leapfrog', *The Economist*, 23 May 2015, http://www.economist.com/news/special-report/21651330-wonders-smart-systems-playing-leapfrog.
8. 'India at crossroads on path to superpower status', *ABC News*, 9 September 2012, http://abcnews.go.com/International/india-crossroads-path-superpower-status/story?id=17173228.

3

Taiwan: A Forgotten Frontier of India's 'Act East'?

Prashant Kumar Singh

The year 2015 marked the 20th anniversary of the establishment of the India-Taipei Association (ITA) in Taiwan and the Taipei Economic and Cultural Centre (TECC) in India. The journey of 20 years now requires stock-taking of the progress and the current state of India-Taiwan relations.[1] This author is of the view that India's investment in relations with Taiwan will innovatively redefine its Act East policy (an evolution from the Look East policy).[2] The underlying assumption here is that India, which aspires for great-power status and a greater role in international affairs, should not uncritically follow the international community's, or for that matter, its own, conventional attitude towards Taiwan. There is enough space within the perimeters of India's support for the People's Republic of China's One-China policy, which obligates countries to recognise Taiwan as a Chinese province, to strengthen relations with Taiwan.

A Case for Enhancing Relations with Taiwan

In September 2015, in an important development, Minister of State for Home Kiren Rijiju, after participating in an event at the North Korean

Embassy in New Delhi on the occasion of North Korea's National Day, made a public announcement that the government had been discussing 'ways and means of upgrading bilateral ties with North Korea'.[3] The statement prompts one to also consider India's relations with another entity in North-East Asia, namely Taiwan. Although India-North Korea relations are not very significant, they still have a framework; whereas India-Taiwan relations do not have a framework.[4] The international community at large, India included, may not recognise the Republic of China (ROC) or Taiwan as a sovereign state. It, nevertheless, remains a territorial and governmental entity in East Asia that operates in the world independently of China. Perhaps the only gap in the entire geographical canvas of India's Act East policy, Taiwan deserves India's attention in this policy. As of now, India does not have any diplomatic relations with Taiwan, nor does it encourage minister and senior official-level visits to Taiwan with some exceptions. Moreover, India hardly expresses its views on issues related to Taiwan. This situation ensures Taiwan's absence in India's vision for its external relations, causing the *unofficial* ties to move at snail's pace and in a somewhat piecemeal fashion.

The current situation provides an opportunity for India to think of ways and means to upgrade its relations with Taiwan without impacting the relations with the PRC. If the present government could bring India-Taiwan relations into a well-defined framework with a long-term vision, it would not only calibrate the Act East policy to a higher level of engagement in East Asia but it would also be yet another example of its attempt to free India's foreign policy from the old ideological remnant.[5] The idea is not to undermine India's support for the PRC's One-China policy but to recast India-Taiwan ties to project India as a serious stakeholder in regional peace, stability and prosperity. The underlying assumption here is that a more constructive, innovative and proactive strategic engagement in Asian affairs would help enhance India's status even if India is not a P-5 power.[6] This is also an opportune time for redefining the relations, as any attempt in this direction would meet with an enthusiastic response from Dr. Tsai Ing-wen of the Democratic Progressive Party (DPP), who is all set to become Taiwan's President on 20 May 2016 after winning the Presidential election in January 2016. She characterises relations with India and ASEAN as a high priority in her new south-bound foreign policy for Taiwan. She also describes India as a pivotal force in her vision for cooperation among democracies in the world.[7]

The proposed relook would have enough justification. Taiwan has thrived as a *de facto* independent governmental entity in the realm of people-to-people relations in the international community despite the PRC's incessant pressure for unification. A full-fledged functional engagement with Taiwan with a long-term vision has a lot to offer to India in the domains of education, science and technology and economy. On a principled note, a mechanical application of the One-China policy,[8] along the lines of the old Communist Party of China (CPC)-Kuomintang (KMT) divide, to post-democratisation Taiwan is unfair. This divide shaped India's position on the Formosa problem in the 1950s like most other countries. (Formosa is a Portuguese name for Taiwan. It remained in international vogue for many centuries. In the 1950s and 1960s, the Formosa problem meant what the Cross-Strait issue is now.) However, the advent of democracy in Taiwan has obliterated the divide. Contrary to KMT's one-party authoritarian rule for around five decades since 1945, present-day democratic Taiwan has multiple voices regarding the Cross-Strait problem. They need to be heard. Besides, Cross-Strait dialogue resumed in 2008 after its breakdown in 1999 and has led to remarkable intensification of cooperation in functional areas such as economy, culture, people-to-people exchanges, and tourism. China has also taken a much more relaxed view of the international community's non-diplomatic economic and cultural engagement with Taiwan. Taiwan has entered the World Health Assembly (WHA) and International Civil Aviation Organisation (ICAO) as an observer during this period. Thus, India's restraint in enhancing engagement with Taiwan is without any substantial reason. A nuanced and imaginative relook at ties with Taiwan will add a distinct flavour of novelty to India's Act East policy, placing it in the league of powers such as the US, Japan and the EU, which have a very substantial cooperative relationship with Taiwan. Moreover, it will help reduce Taiwan's sense of isolation and contribute to its confidence to negotiate peace and stability in Cross-Strait relations.

Picking up the Threads from History

Contrary to what the silence and mutual oblivion of four decades after India switched its diplomatic recognition from the ROC to the PRC in 1949 might suggest, India in the 1950s and 1960s was not reticent about the Formosa problem. It is true that contrary to his previously famous congeniality and bonhomie with Generalissimo Chiang Kai-shek and his family, Nehru's views on him and the KMT government hardened due to Chiang's attempts to undermine, in Nehru's view, peace efforts in the Korea War (1950-53) and his refusal to recognise the changed course of history. Nevertheless, he was closely following the Formosa problem in order to take an objective view of it. Formosa was equally an object of ideological interest for many opposition parties and leaders in India, who offered their critique of Nehru's China policy and his non-aligned foreign policy, citing his government's stand on Formosa.

Although India had no space to play any conciliatory role in the Formosa problem unlike the Korean issue because both the PRC and the ROC were vehemently opposed to any international mediation in the problem,[9] Nehru did take a stand and cogently expressed India's position on Formosa. He had opposed international intervention in the Chinese civil war, arguing that the world should await the verdict of the Chinese people.[10] His government switched the diplomatic recognition, maintaining that 'as for recognition, there is no doubt that recognition has to be given to a fact'.[11] Once the fact that the PRC had been founded and had effective control on mainland China was established with maximum certitude, his government recognised it as the sole Chinese state in the historical and civilisational continuum of China and accepted Taiwan as historically a Chinese territory. Although his government agreed that the Formosa problem was a continuation of the civil war, it was opposed to the problem being left to the two belligerents to resolve it through military methods, as the problem had been aligned with the superpower rivalry after the outbreak of the Korea War. The Indian government advocated for a negotiated settlement through political means under the UN principles. India as part of the three-member group along with Iran and Canada, was for negotiating the ceasefire in the Korean peninsula and for setting up a body comprising the representatives of the UK, the US, the USSR and the PRC to resolve all the Far Eastern problems in accordance with the UN principles, including the Formosa problem, which had potentially grave implications for world peace.[12] Even though the Nehru government accepted Taiwan as historically a Chinese territory, it acknowledged that Taiwan had acquired a 'distinct individuality' in the course of history (an allusion to the five-decades-long Japanese rule in Taiwan) and saw the prospect of autonomy for Taiwan.[13]

Nehru also voiced his concerns during the first Taiwan Strait crisis (1954-55) and the second Taiwan Strait crisis (1958) in Parliament and outside. The two crises were about the control over offshore islands lying between the PRC and the ROC and held by the KMT forces. During the second crisis, Nehru exchanged correspondence with British Prime Minister Harold Macmillan regarding the crisis. He was of the view that from a security point of view, the islands should have been under the PRC's possession as they were vital for its security due to their geographical proximity with the mainland. However, the Taiwan issue was a separate and larger political problem which needed more time for its resolution.[14]

The Indian government was generally not heard on the Formosa problem or in general about Taiwan after 1958, a feature that characterises India-Taiwan ties at present too. This was the time when India's own relations with the PRC were taking a bitter turn, eventually culminating in the 1962 war.

In addition to Prime Minister Nehru, many opposition leaders showed an equal interest in Formosa. They included Ram Manohar Lohia, the socialist leader, J.B. Kripalani and Ashok Mehta of the Praja Socialist Party (PSP), M.R. Masani of the Swatantra Party, Balraj Madhok of the Jan Sangh, and V.G. Deshpande and N.B. Khare of the Hindu Mahasabha. Congress parliamentarians such as Ila Pal Choudhury and M.K. Krishna too had their views on Formosa divergent from the government. Many of the opposition leaders were formerly in Nehru's Congress Party and had criticised his policies on China and Formosa. The essence of their critique was that the government demonstrated double standards as it recognised the effective possession of Communist China on the mainland but not of Nationalist China on Taiwan. The Nationalists' effective possession of Taiwan was as much a fact as the Communists' effective possession of mainland China. The Indian government fought communists at home (an allusion to the armed communist rebellions in some parts of India after independence) but was supporting them internationally. It ignored the Formosans' right to self-determination and did not appreciate Formosa's strategic value vis-à-vis communist China. These opposition leaders even pitched for diplomatic recognition for the ROC. They had been criticising Nehru almost since the switch of the recognition, particularly after the PRC's march into Tibet in 1950. Their criticism grew louder after the 1962 War.[15]

Nehru, however, correctly recognised that the course of history was against ROC. The opposition also ignored the repressive nature of the KMT regime in Taiwan. The Chiang Kai-shek government was staunchly opposed to simultaneous recognition of the PRC and the ROC. Besides, the Taiwan government had the same understanding on the Sino-Indian border dispute as the mainland government.

A recently published book, *India and Taiwan: From Benign Neglect to Pragmatism* (edited by D.P. Tripathi and B.R. Deepak, Vij Books, New Delhi, 2016) informs in its introductory chapter, on the basis of Zhao Weiwen's *Records of Turbulences in Sino-Indian Relations: 1949-1999* (in Chinese; Current Affairs Press, Beijing), that quite a few governmental, including military, parliamentary and media exchanges between India and Taiwan took place in the 1960s. This information changes the commonly held perception that there was total silence between India and Taiwan till the early 1990s after India switched the recognition. Nevertheless, this information does not alter the understanding of the course of India-Taiwan relations, as the activities in the 1960s did not change India's essential policy towards the PRC and Taiwan.[16]

Newly independent India had a clear thinking on Taiwan and the Cross-Strait problem at the time when it was a weak country. Now India is a much more assured country in terms of national power and is far more active in East Asia, but it hardly expresses any views about Taiwan and the Cross-Strait issue. Some vital facts concerning Taiwan and Cross-Strait relations have changed since 1949, and Taiwan has shown tenacity to sustain itself as an entity separate from the PRC. The CPC-KMT frame of the problem is no longer relevant. The international community's non-appreciation of the changed frame of Cross-Strait relations and a mechanical adherence to the PRC's One-China policy amounts to intercession and exerting weight on behalf of China in Cross-Strait relations, which goes against Nehru's principled opposition to international interference in the Chinese people's affairs.

Present State of India-Taiwan Ties

So far, the nature of India's ties with Taiwan has been in tune with the mainstream international community's conventional attitude towards Taiwan, which adheres to the PRC's claim over Taiwan. The PRC insists that countries wanting to have diplomatic relations with it must acknowledge that there is only 'One China' that is PRC, the ROC no longer exists and Taiwan is a province of China. It does not object to countries having economic and cultural relations with Taiwan but takes umbrage to political relations in any semblance, and any signs that may be construed as recognising Taiwan's sovereignty. As of today, only 22 small Central American, African and Pacific countries, and also the Holy See, recognise the ROC diplomatically. Taiwan conducts its relations with members of the international community in a non-diplomatic and non-sovereign fashion through its offices under various nomenclatures, generally terming them as economic and cultural centres. Similarly, India conducts transactions with Taiwan through the quasi-official ITA, and its Taiwanese counterpart TECC. Incidentally, the Indian Ministry of External Affairs (MEA) website does not mention Taiwan.

India approaching Taiwan for investment in the early 1990s, followed by the establishment of *unofficial* relations in the mid-1990s, could be considered an outcome of its then unfolding Look East policy.[17] However, the scale and intensity of the relations have all along been so low that the ties with Taiwan do not demonstrate any effective application of the Look East or Act East policy. If we compare India's relations with China, Japan and South Korea with those with Taiwan, it is evident that Taiwan is off the radar of its Act East policy.

Mapping the Present State of the Relations

India unqualifiedly severed relations with the ROC in 1949, and did not maintain institutionalised contacts with the Nationalist government in any form. The establishment of the ITA and TECC was a beginning from scratch. However, in spite of the late beginning and odd nature of the relations, the ties have registered noticeable growth. India had (US)$6.2 billion trade with Taiwan in FY 2014-15. The bilateral trade reached a record high of $8 billion in 2011-12. The growth is remarkable considering the 1999 figure of $984 million. Although cumulative Taiwanese foreign direct investment (FDI) was only $99.78 million (0.04% of total FDI) in June 2015,[18] India has received investment from Taiwan's big-ticket companies such as China Steel Corporation and Continental Engineering Corp. They have concluded core agreements, such as double taxation avoidance agreement and Admission Temporary Admission (ATA) Carnet Protocol, for trade promotion. A memorandum of understanding (MoU) between India's Department of Science and Technology (DST) under the Ministry of Science and Technology and Taiwan's National Science Council, signed in 2007, is a significant pointer of progress in the relations. Under the MoU, the two sides have had scientific exchanges since 2007. Recently, India has granted E-Visa facility for the Taiwanese to visit India. Remarkably, educational exchanges have emerged as the mainstay of India-Taiwan people-to-people contacts. Various universities such as the Indian Institutes of Technology (IITs), University of Delhi (DU) and Jawaharlal Nehru University (JNU) in India and the National Chiao Tung University (NCTU), National Tsing Hua University (NTHU) and National Chengchi University (NCCU) in Taiwan are having exchange programmes with each other. The Association of Indian Universities (AIU) has extended its recognition to the degrees granted by Taiwanese universities. Low-key but growing dialogue between their larger strategic communities involving think-tanks and universities is equally notable.[19]

Progress, but Piecemeal

These instances do point out some progress in the bilateral relations. However, on the whole, the plot and the canvas of the relations remain thin and narrow. Progress has remained slow, piecemeal and a sum of sporadic initiatives without any long-term vision. Governmental frameworks for promoting people-to-people contacts in business, culture and education are not really many.

Graph 1: India's Trade with Taiwan (in US$ billion)

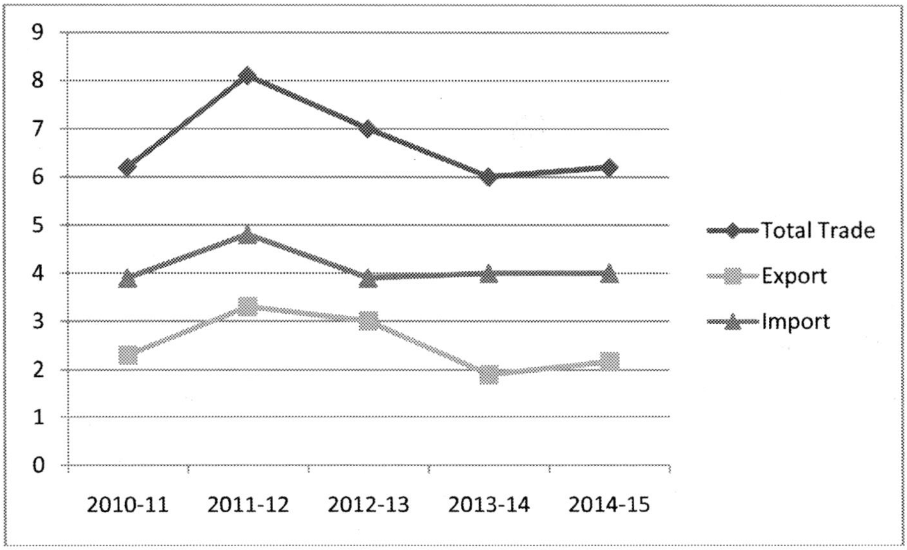

Source: Based on data from Department of Commerce, EXIM Bank, India.

Another notable lacuna in the relations is the absence of high (minister or secretary) level official visits, though visits by Taiwanese ministers to India have occasionally taken place. Taiwan's Education Minister Dr. Wu Ching-ji visited India in 2011. From the Indian side, additional secretary-level officials from select ministries such as the Ministry of Science and Technology and Ministry of Information Technology perhaps remain the highest ranking officials to have visited Taiwan.[20]

There has also been news about Taiwanese companies facing difficulties in India because of automatic extension of rules that are applicable to Chinese companies to Taiwanese companies.[21] Taiwan's Continental Engineering Corporation (CEC), involved in the Delhi Metro project, complained in 2013 how it was being asked to seek prior approval for bringing capital each time under the Reserve Bank of India (RBI) rules applicable to China. The use of the phrase 'Taiwan, Province of China' or 'Chinese Taipei' in Indian official documents combined with the use of the word 'China' in the names of some Taiwanese companies creates confusion about the identity of the Taiwanese companies. Taiwanese tourists have reportedly faced difficulties in India for similar reasons too. It is not very clear whether India finds a free trade agreement (FTA) with Taiwan commercially unattractive or it has concerns about the Chinese reaction. The Indian Council for Research on International Economic Relations (ICRIER) and Taiwan's Chung-Hua Institution for Economic Research (CIER) have carried out a joint study for the FTA.

This study was announced by the then Foreign Secretary Nirupama Rao in 2011.[22] This announcement and later India agreeing for the Taiwanese President Ma Ying-jeou's stopover in Mumbai in 2012[23] and Vice-President Wu Den-yih's layover in New Delhi in 2014[24] kindled hope for upgrading of the ties. However, these developments have not produced any new pattern or led to any new breakthrough in relations calibrating the Act East policy.

One could argue that India-Taiwan ties have only a limited mandate in conformity with the support for the PRC's One-China policy. However, when compared to the depth of engagement of powers such as the US, Japan and the EU with Taiwan, it is clear that even the limited scope is under-realised.[25] US, Japan and EU relations with Taiwan include advanced areas of cooperation such as visawaiver, extradition treaty, judicial exchanges, cooperation against international terrorism, nuclear security, environment and human rights dialogue and consultation, in addition to normal trade and investment and educational exchanges. It is seen from Tables 1 and 2 and Graph 2 that the One-China policy is not impacting Taiwan's people-to-people relations with the international community. Thus, the bar for India-Taiwan ties appears to be too low. China's singling out India's deepening of functional relations with Taiwan cannot go far considering its approval of Taiwan's deep cooperative relations with other major players in the international community.

Explaining the Absence of a Long-term Vision for the Relations

More than fear of Chinese reaction, the low scale of India-Taiwan bilateral relations is actually because Taiwan is not receiving enough attention from the political and MEA's top leadership in India. This might be partly on account of concerns about the Chinese reaction, partly from unawareness and lack of interest in Taiwanese affairs, at least in the political leadership, and partly from entrenched bureaucratic habits. Not many in India are

Table 1: Select Indicators of Taiwan's Integration with the World

Year	Indicator	Global Rank/Absolute Figure
2014	Foreign Exchange Reserves	5th
2014	Exporter of Merchandise	20th
2014	Importer of merchandise	18th
2014	Exporter of commercial services	23rd
2014	Importer of Commercial services	29th
2014	Trade volume	US$ 587.73 billion
2014	Outward FDI	US$ 17.12 billion
2012	US patents to Taiwanese citizens	11, 624 with 5th rank and 4.20% of total patents
2015	Universities in top 500	11
2014	Visa-free entry or landing visa	Around 140 countries

Note: The outward FDI data is the combined data of Taiwanese FDI in China ($9.83 billion) and in other countries ($7.29 billion). As for US patents, Taiwan has maintained the rank and the percentage share with progressive increase in absolute numbers since 2009, as per the available data.

Sources: For data on foreign exchange reserves, export and import in merchandise and commercial services, trade volume and FDI, 'Economy and Finance', *The Republic of China Yearbook 2015*, at http://www.ey.gov.tw/en/cp.aspx?n=7A3C3FFB6914DBB8(accessed 10 March, 2016); For the patent data, Table 8, 2013 Industrial Development in Taiwan, R.O.C. (PDF Version), at http://www.moeaidb.gov.tw/external/view/en/about/index01.html#table_8 (accessed 29 September 2015). For the university ranking data, Webometrics Ranking of World Universities at http://www.webometrics.info/en/Asia/Taiwan (accessed 30 September 2015).
'140 countries now offer visa-free treatment for Taiwan nationals', *Want China Times*, 21 May 2014, at http://www.wantchinatimes.com/news-subclass-cnt.aspx?id=20140521000082&cid=1101 (accessed 7 October 2014).

very clear about the dynamics of Cross-Strait relations and Taiwan's domestic scenario.

Taiwan should also share the blame for the insipid state of relations. Taiwan's governments, particularly after 2000, have swung to extreme priorities: robust foreign relations under the DPP government led by Chen Shui-bian (2000-08) and good relations with mainland China under the KMT government in Taiwan led by President Ma Ying-jeou (2008-16). This swing is also reflected in its relations with India. The DPP government showed a strong political interest in India, though heightened Cross-Strait tensions at the time did not allow India to reciprocate its overtures. In

Table 2: Select Benchmarks of Taiwan's Global Competitiveness

Institute	Assessment	Year	World Ranking
Heritage Foundation	Index of Economic Freedom	2016	14
International Institute for Management Development (IMD)	World Competitiveness	2015	11
Business Environment Risk Intelligence (BERI)	Profit Opportunity Recommendation	2013	3
	Operations Risk Index		2
	Political Risk Index		10th lowest political risk in the world
	Remittance and Repatriation Factor		1
World Economic Forum (WEF)	Global Competitiveness Entrepreneurship Index Product Innovation Process Innovation	2013	12 1 1 3
Economic Intelligence Unit (EIU)	Information Technology Industry Competitiveness Index	2011	13

Source: http://www.heritage.org/index/ranking; http://www.imd.org/uupload/imd.website/wcc/scoreboard.pdf; http://investtaiwan.nat.gov.tw/eng/show.jsp?ID=3; http://globalindex11.bsa.org/key-findings/ (accessed 25 April, 2016)

Graph 2: Taiwan's Top Trading Partners in US$ billion (January-December 2015)

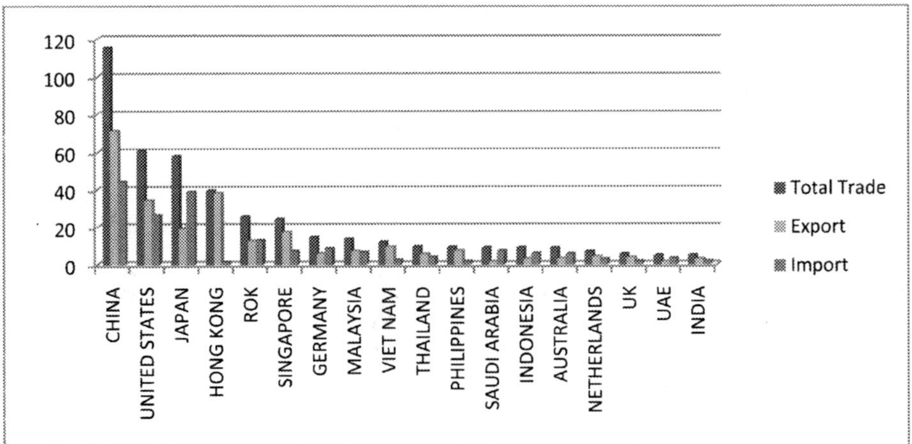

Source: Based on trade statistics provided by Taiwan's Bureau of Foreign Trade at http://cus93.trade.gov.tw/ENGLISH/FSCE/

fact, the DPP's idea of an India-Taiwan-Japan triangle was considered too provocative not only for China, but also within Taiwan. Contrary to this, the outgoing KMT government has pursued good relations with India but without articulating an India-specific political vision. This situation leads to inconsistency and difference in intensity in initiatives. Taiwan needs to correct this, and take a balanced and measured view as to what exactly it expects from India.[26]

Summing Up

Progress in India-Taiwan relations is inevitably linked with the state of Cross-Strait relations. Fishing in troubled waters is not India's policy, nor is it feasible for India to create a balance-of-power context vis-à-vis China involving Taiwan. Cross-Strait relations are a 'knot' essentially between China, Taiwan and the US. India will never like to play the role of interloper. The incoming DPP government should realise that the best way to upgrade relations with India is to do so in the positive territory of relations with realistic limits. India can have a strategic partnership with Taiwan for people-to-people relations only, and not in the conventionally understood meaning of the term.

On its part, India should realise that Taiwan deserves greater attention from India for cooperation and collaboration because in spite of its difficult diplomatic and political predicament, tiny Taiwan, well-integrated with the international community, is an island of opportunities in economy, education and scientific innovation. Being essentially a part of the Chinese civilisation, Taiwan provides an alternative window to Chinese culture, civilisation, society and language other than the PRC. Enhanced cooperative relations with it are in India's interest.

What is needed is a realistic and self-sustaining framework for India-Taiwan relations to tap their full potential of functional ties in trade and investment, science and technological collaboration and civil exchanges. This needs to be an all-encompassing and comprehensive framework for people-to-people relations covering every aspect and dimension of relations that any set of two people can have. Considering the quantum of trade of the two sides (India's $992.3 billion in 2015 and Taiwan's $587.73 billion in 2014), India-Taiwan trade has the potential to grow further. As seen in

Table 1, there is considerable scope for boosting Taiwanese investment in India. Taiwan, which visualises itself as an exporter of Chinese culture, can play an important role in building Chinese-speaking human resources in India. Scholarly, parliamentary, civil society, and track 1 and track 1.5 exchanges can contribute to India's better understanding of Chinese culture and civilisation and society. Being kindred and with easy access to mainland Chinese society and state, Taiwan can help India better understand the society and system in the PRC. In return, deepened engagement with India will ensure reciprocal material benefits and aspirational gains for Taiwan. India can contribute to help Taiwan reduce its sense of isolation and gain confidence to negotiate with China. The two sides should produce a model framework for people-to-people relations which has emulative value for the countries that are not Taiwan's diplomatic partners nor have historically strong ties with Taiwan like the US and Japan. It might inspire their interest in peace and stability in Taiwan Strait.

Finally, with a view to enhancing bilateral ties, India can seek to undertake measures that would help it build a framework for its relations with Taiwan as well as further its Act East policy. India should come up with a policy/position paper for India-Taiwan ties, drawing insights from how the US, Japan, EU and other major countries are conducting their relations with Taiwan within the perimeter of their support for the PRC's One-China policy. ITA and TECC should consider signing a partnership vision document providing direction, articulating norms and setting objectives and goals for India-Taiwan relations. The government should issue directives to ministries, agencies and departments explaining India's position on Taiwan and directing them how to conduct business with it with mutual benefits in view. India should let its views be known on issues pertaining to Taiwan, such as Taiwan's entry to Regional Comprehensive Economic Partnership (RCEP), Asian Infrastructure Investment Bank (AIIB) and specialised UN agencies, through MEA officials, on their merit. The views might be of academic importance only. However, India should let others know what it thinks of those issues. Representatives of the two countries should be encouraged to discuss issues in the multilateral organisations in which Taiwan is present as observer. A robust and expansive consultative mechanism across the governmental spans should be established with the objectives of exchanging views and information and identifying sectors for cooperation and collaboration. With the possible exception of the MEA, Ministry of Defence and Ministry of Home Affairs, India should consider allowing minister-level visits to Taiwan. While visits by cabinet ministers might wait for some time, minister-of-state level and secretary-level visits to Taiwan may be encouraged immediately. Chief Ministers may also be encouraged to explore trade and investment in Taiwan. Parliamentary exchanges, which do not represent the executive arm of the system, are also a good alternative for reaching out to each other. There should be investment in building scholarly and diplomatic expertise on Taiwan, Cross-Strait relations and Taiwan's place in Asia-Pacific.

NOTES

1. This chapter has drawn on the author's monograph, *Transforming India-Taiwan Relations: New Perspectives*, IDSA Monograph Series, No. 35, April 2014: pp. 1-156.
2. The Look East policy, after the end of the Cold War, aimed at enhancing India's relations with the East Asian countries, particularly in trade and investment. Many of these countries had been in the US camp during the Cold War and had lacklustre relations with India, who was perceived to be sympathetic towards the USSR-led socialist block. In the decades after the early 1990s, the policy has come to cover political, economic, cultural and defence aspects of the relations bilaterally and multilaterally. The Modi government in 2014 renamed it as the Act East policy, conveying India's aim to deepen its approach in the strategic realm of the region.
3. Kallol Bhattacherjee, 'India Reaches Out, Wants to Upgrade Ties with North Korea', *The Hindu*, 16 September 2015, at http://www.thehindu.com/news/national/india-reaches-out-wants-to-upgrade-ties-with-north-korea/article7656332.ece (accessed 29 September 2015); Prashant Kumar Singh, 'North Korea: An Advance Frontier of India's "Act East"?', Special Feature, IDSA, 1 December 2015, at http://idsa.in/specialfeature/north-korea-indias-act-east_psingh_011215 (Accessed 1 May 2016).
4. The *ground-rules* by the ITA in 1995 that laid emphasis on not conferring any sign of sovereignty on Taiwan in carrying out its function, were about ensuring that India's support for the PRC's One-China policy is not undermined. They were not a framework for India-Taiwan relations as such. 'The India-Taipei Association: A Mission Extraordinaire', Interview with Ambassador Vinod C. Khanna, *Indian Foreign Affairs Journal*, Vol. 5, No. 2, April 2010: pp. 240-51.
5. The Modi government has shown its inclination to inject even greater pragmatism into India's foreign policy, as seen in its decision to have regular Japanese participation in the Indo-US MALABAR naval exercise. The increasing pragmatism has been seen in Indo-US relations too. The two governments have jointly pledged support for freedom of navigation in their joint communiqués. Currently, India and the US are negotiating an agreement for sharing of military logistics — The Logistics Exchange Memorandum of Agreement (LEMOA).

6. Prashant Kumar Singh, 'North Korea: An Advance Frontier of India's "Act East"?', n. 3.
7. 'DPP 29th Anniversary Diplomatic Reception', 22 September 2015, at http://english.dpp.org.tw/dpp-29th-anniversary/ (accessed 8 October 2015). For detailed discussion, see Prashant Kumar Singh, *Transforming India-Taiwan Relations: New Perspectives*, n. 1, pp. 89-97 and pp. 113-117.
8. The Cross-Strait problem has persisted since 1949 when the defeated KMT retreated to the island of Taiwan, which imperial Qing China had ceded to imperial Japan under the treaty of Shimonoseki after the Qing defeat in the Sino-Japanese War in 1895. The island returned to the Republic of China (ROC) in 1945 after Japan's defeat in World War II. Technically, the civil war is yet to be formally terminated. The two sides have denied each other's legal existence and legitimacy to rule. While the PRC does not accept the existence of the ROC, the ROC constitution still claims jurisdiction over entire China. They have their own version of the One-China policy, meaning that China is one (for the Communists, the PRC; and for the KMT, the ROC) and Taiwan is its part. This One-China, Respective interpretations (also known as the 1992 Consensus) became the basis of Cross-Strait rapprochement which began in 1992. However, democratisation in Taiwan in the 1990s has given a new twist to this general situation. The Democratic Progressive Party (DPP), which was in power from 2000-08, and has again won the Presidential election in January 2016, considers Taiwan as a victim of alien Chinese civil war, sees Taiwan independent of China, does not recognise the 1992 Consensus, and maintains that the fate of Taiwan (read unification or independence) will be decided by the will of the Taiwanese people. However, it too is constrained by the ROC constitution. Because of its opposition to the 1992 Consensus, the PRC refuses to accept the DPP as a dialogue partner in the Cross-Strait issue. Incidentally, the Cross-Strait dialogue under Lee Teng-hui-led KMT government broke down in 1999 and was resumed in 2008 after Ma Ying-jeou became President in 2008. To better understand Cross-Strait relations, see Richard C. Bush, *Untying the Knot: Making Peace in the Taiwan Strait*, Brooking Institution Press, Washington D.C., 2005; and Su Chi, *Taiwan's Relations with Mainland China: A Tail Wagging Two Dogs*, Routledge, London/New York, 2010.
9. India was a member in the United Nations Temporary Commission on Korea in 1947 for elections in Korea. It chaired the Neutral Nations' Repatriation Commission during the Korea War (1950-53).
10. Jawaharlal Nehru, 'Letter', 15 August 1949, in *Letters to Chief Ministers*, G. Parthasarathi (ed.), Teen Murti House, New Delhi, Volume 1, 1985, p. 434.
11. 'To Tan Yun-shan', Letter, *Selected Works of Jawaharlal Nehru* (*SWJN*), Second Series, Vol. 14 (part 1), Teen Murti House, New Delhi, 1992, pp. 514-515. Tan Yun-shan was a Chinese scholar at Santiniketan in West Bengal, India.
12. J.P. Jain, 'The Legal Status of Formosa: A Study of British, Chinese and Indian Views', *The American Journal of International Law*, 57 (1): 39-40.
13. 'To Chief Ministers', Letter, 6 September 1958, *SWJN*, Second Series, Vol. 44, Teen Murti House, New Delhi, 2012, p. 2.
14. 'To Harold Macmillan', Letter, 7 September 1958, *SWJN*, Second Series, Vol. 44, Teen Murti House, New Delhi, 2012, p. 573.

15. Nancy Jetly, *India-China Relations, 1947-77: A Study of Parliament's Role in the Making of Foreign Policy*, Radiant Publishers, New Delhi, 1979. The book contains important references about Formosa that figured in the Indian parliamentary debates in the 1950s and 1960s. The author has used these references from the perspective of India-Taiwan relations in *Transforming India-Taiwan Relations: New Perspectives*, n. 1, pp. 53-60.
16. The author has perused the introduction of the book available at www.amazon.in in kindle book format. The information opens an interesting area of research. The research would require knowing whether they were just a kneejerk response to the defeat at the hand of China in 1962 or were they exploring some strategic equation with Taiwan? Also, to what extent did they have the government's backing? What was the Chiang Kai-shek government's response to India after the 1962 war and towards these initiatives? These questions need to be probed from Indian sources. These moves went nowhere as the tide of time was against the ROC. The ROC lost the China seat in the UNSC in 1971 and then the US recognition in 1979. But Taiwan chose to remain in the US camp. India continued to subscribe to the PRC's One-China policy. It did not change even its essential Tibet policy in spite of having far greater leverage in the Tibetan Government in Exile (TGIE) being based in India. Later in the 1980s, as Fang Tien-Sze informs, Vincent C. Siewm, Taiwan's former Vice President, had tried to apply for visa to visit India seven times when he served as the Director-General, Bureau of Foreign Trade, Ministry of Economic Affairs (1982–88), but was refused. Fang Tien-Sze, 'Taiwan's Relations with India: Issues and Trends', *China Report*, 49 (4), 2013: p. 428.
17. For details, see Parris H. Chang, 'From Benign Neglect to Pragmatism: The Political and Security Issues between Taiwan and India', *Think India Journal*, Vol. 16, December 2013, PP. 74-78; Prashant Kumar Singh, *Transforming India-Taiwan Relations: New Perspectives*, n. 1, pp. 86-89.
18. Fact Sheet on Foreign Direct Investment (FD), From April 2000 to June 2015, at http://dipp.nic.in/English/Publications/FDI_Statistics/2015/india_FDI_June2015.pdf (Accessed 1 May 2016).
19. Prashant Kumar Singh, *Transforming India-Taiwan Relations: New Perspectives*, n. 1, pp. 90-92, 97-104, and 113-117.
20. High-level political visits or cabinet-ranking leaders' visits to Taiwan are a tricky issue internationally. For example, from the US, there have been a few intermittent cabinet-ranking visits to Taiwan. The same is true for countries such as the UK and Australia. However, official-level visits, particularly between Taiwan and the US, have been regular and extensive. See Shirley A. Kan and Wayne M. Morrison, *U.S.-Taiwan Relationship: Overview of Policy Issues*, Monograph, Congressional Research Service (CRS), December 2014, pp. 14-16, at https://www.fas.org/sgp/crs/row/R41952.pdf (accessed 7 October 2014).
21. 'Taiwan Raises Issue with India over Investments', *Taipei Times*, 19 July 2013, at http://www.taipeitimes.com/News/taiwan/archives/2013/07/19/2003567675 (accessed 7 October 2013).
22. 'Not yet time to conduct official FTA talks with India: MOEA', Focus Taiwan News Channel, 8 March 2011, at http://bilaterals.org/spip.php?page=print&id_article=19184 (accessed 29 September 2015). The news item contains information about Foreign Secretary Rao's announcement.

23. 'Taiwan President Makes Surprise Stopover in Mumbai', *Times of India*, 8 April 2012, at timesofindia.indiatimes.com/city/mumbai/Taiwan—makes-surprise-stopover-in-Mumbai/articleshow/12582698.cms (accessed 29 September 2015).
24. 'Vice-President Wu Den-yih's Layover in New Delhi in 2014, China Likely to Bristle', *Times of India*, 26 April 2014, at http://timesofindia.indiatimes.com/india/Taiwan-vice-president-to-land-in-Delhi-China-likely-to-bristle/articleshow/34220575.cms (accessed 29 September 2014).
25. For the extent and depth of US-Taiwan relations, see information available at the website of the American Institute in Taiwan (AIT), the de facto embassy of the US in Taiwan, at www.ait.org.tw/en/ait-tecro-agreements.html (accessed 7 October 2015); Shirley A. Kan and Wayne M. Morrison, *U.S.-Taiwan Relationship: Overview of Policy Issues*, Monograph, Congressional Research Service (CRS), December 2014, at https://www.fas.org/sgp/crs/row/R41952.pdf (accessed 7 October 2014). For the EU-Taiwan engagement, see 'EU-Taiwan Fact File 2015', http://eeas.europa.eu/delegations/taiwan/documents/more_info/eufactfile2015.pdf (accessed 7 October 2015). The EU has a dialogue and exchange programme for Taiwan in areas such as environment, nuclear security and human rights. For Japan's relations with Taiwan, see 'Recent Japan-Taiwan Relations and the Taiwan Situation', July 2013, Ministry of Foreign Affairs of Japan, at http://www.mofa.go.jp/region/asia-paci/taiwan/pdfs/japan-taiwan_relations.pdf (accessed 7 October 2015).
26. Prashant Kumar Singh, *Transforming India-Taiwan Relations: New Perspectives*, n. 1, pp. 92-98, 110-17.

4

India-Taiwan Relations: Constrained or Self-Constraining?

Jabin T. Jacob

The big problem in India-Taiwan relations is the lack of ambition. Given the depth of economic relations and often enough, of political ties too, that many countries including in East Asia itself have with Taiwan, one wonders if there is not also a lack of creativity in the case of India-Taiwan ties. The economic dimension in the relationship is often highlighted – the most recent case being the announcement in August 2015 of Foxconn investing (US) $5 billion in India[1]—but it also seems unlikely that the Government of India went out of its way to court Foxconn because it was a Taiwanese company or indeed, that it is going out of its way for any Taiwanese company. If the Act East policy is an opportunity to recast and revitalise India's ties with East Asia across dimensions, then this recasting and revitalisation must also cover Taiwan.

One-China Policy

If the development of China-Taiwan relations in the decades following China's economic opening up and reforms is any indication, the story of India-Taiwan relations is one of missed opportunities. This is understandable in some respects, given that India-China relations themselves were only slowly recovering from the 1962 conflict. The 1980s were still early days as negotiations on the boundary dispute were taking off. Still, India took note of Taiwan under the Look East policy fairly early, as indicated by the 1995 establishment of representative offices in Taipei and in New Delhi.

Nevertheless, relations have remained largely constrained as this period also marks the beginning of the inexorable rise of China and the implicit consequent pressure on the development of India-Taiwan ties. Given the importance of Taiwan's enterprises in pushing forward China-Taiwan ties, the flip side of India's lagging behind China in economic growth and openness was that the same driver was not available for India-Taiwan relations.

While the beginning of talks on a bilateral Comprehensive Economic Partnership Agreement in the mid-2000s highlighted the importance to India of Taiwan's economy and its investments, on the political front, matters have remained more or less frozen.

From the time that the first NDA government came to power in New Delhi, there has been an uptick in dialogues and exchanges between think-tanks and sections of government on the two sides mostly related to foreign policy and security issues. However, these interactions have been sporadic, ad hoc and sometimes were also discouraged by sections within the Government of India itself. While there have been unofficial exchanges between the militaries and delegations led by military officials, in India these are not publicised and often not even to scholars and researchers in the universities and think-tanks.

Such diffidence or, perhaps, excessive caution, on the Indian side is without question a result of New Delhi's one-China policy. That for India, the one-China policy resulted in such diffidence or caution should be a matter of concern not so much for the Taiwanese but from the perspective of Indian national interests. It would not be a stretch to say that the Chinese themselves are surprised at India's hesitant pace of expansion of its economic and political interests with Taiwan. If most other countries in East Asia, including those immediately neighbouring China, have robust economic ties with Taiwan as well as significant people-to-people movements and interactions, it is a wonder why India with its difficult relationship with China does not/did not interact more closely with Taiwan at multiple levels.

When the new NDA regime came to power, there appeared to be some rethink on the one-China policy, with the new Prime Minister Narendra Modi inviting both Lobsang Sangay, the Tibetan Sikyong and Tien Chung-kwang, the Representative of the Taipei Economic and Cultural Center (TECC), which is Taiwan's unofficial embassy in India, to attend his swearing-in ceremony in May 2014. Later, in September the same year, the Indian Minister for External Affairs, Sushma Swaraj, went on record at her first formal media interaction stating that the Chinese Foreign Minister was told during his visit to New Delhi that 'If we believe in one China policy, you should also believe in one India policy.' She went on to add in response to another question, 'When [the Chinese] raised with us the issue of Tibet and Taiwan, we appreciated their sensitivities. So we also want that they should understand and appreciate our sensitivities regarding Arunachal.'[2] Interestingly, Swaraj did not mention Pakistan-Occupied Kashmir, which would have been the more appropriate equivalence than Arunachal, which is, in any case, under Indian administration. The fact that Tibet and Taiwan were mentioned in the same breath should not lead to the conclusion that the Indian government thinks that Taiwan is as important as Tibet is in its foreign policy and security calculations. It is in effect a lack of understanding of the nature of China-Taiwan ties that led the minister to stop at only mentioning Arunachal.[3]

However, quite apart from the issue of the one-China policy, it is also important to remember that Taiwan is not a 'small' country, even if in area it is smaller than Bhutan. It is from many perspectives virtually a 'middle power', with a population greater than about three-quarters of the world's countries, a substantial military, an advanced economy, and foreign exchange reserves larger than those of India.[4] It is, thus, doubly a failure of Indian imagination and policy that the relationship with Taiwan remains as underdeveloped as it is today.

The Taiwan-China Relationship: Signposts for India

Over the years, the Communist Party of China (CPC)-ruled mainland has adopted a variety of approaches to bring Taiwan – dubbed a 'renegade province' – around. While for most of the Maoist and Dengist eras, there were really no serious attempts at coercion, rapprochement with the US in 1971 did give a fillip to the one-China policy, advantaging the People's Republic that put the Republic of China in Taiwan on a very shaky footing as far as its international standing was concerned.

As the Dengist era wound down and China became increasingly confident of its economic growth and global political profile, it also seemed to get increasingly impatient about reunification. The run-up to Taiwan's first free and fair elections for the presidency in 1996 resulted in the Chinese shelling the Taiwan Strait as a warning against independence. When the US intervened with a show of force of its own, sending its aircraft carrier into the waters between China and Taiwan, Beijing learned its lessons and began adopting more nuanced political approaches based on the economic reality of growing economic interdependence between the two entities.[5] It must be noted that India and Taiwan decided to set up their representative offices in 1995 before Taiwan's first democratic elections. For New Delhi, this was perhaps of a piece with its Look East policy but also part of a realist turn in its policies that was reflected also in its rapprochement with the military junta in Myanmar in the same period.

Lee Teng-hui, the 1996 presidential election winner, was also the first native-born Taiwanese to hold the office. While Lee encouraged the idea of Taiwan as a separate state, the KMT itself remained devoted to the idea of reunification.[6] This period also saw the rise of the Democratic Progressive Party (DPP) that called for complete independence and stressed a separate and unique Taiwanese identity. This trend was continued with the election of the DPP's Chen Shui-bian as president in 2000 and 2004. The year 2004 also saw the launch of the first official scholarships for Indian students by the Taiwanese Ministry of Foreign Affairs administered through the TECC in New Delhi. These scholarships have continued, no doubt for strategic reasons even though India has naturally not reciprocated.

Once again returning to threatening Taiwan, the Hu Jintao administration in China came up with the Anti-Secession Law in 2005 that virtually guaranteed the use of force as a legal obligation in case Taiwan declared independence. By this time, however, the Taiwanese businesses and economic elites were heavily dependent on China for their economic well-being and ordinary Taiwanese also seemed largely uncomfortable with the DPP's apparently reckless provocation of Beijing. The corruption scandals swirling around the Chen Shui-bian administration did not help and the KMT returned to the presidency under Ma Ying-jeou. Thus began a period of still closer economic linkages and increasing international space for Taiwan – China stopped poaching from the few countries that still accorded Taiwan diplomatic recognition.

The major losses suffered by the KMT in the nine-in-one local elections – called so because elections were held to nine levels of local government – at the end of November 2014 must have caused China to rethink the scope and recalibrate the pace of its embrace of the island. These elections to city and local governments included 22 seats for city mayors, of which the KMT won only six and three of them by only the thinnest of margins, while the opposition DPP won 13, in addition to supporting several winning independent candidates.[7] The KMT's loss six years after Ma rode to power was due to both internal and external reasons. But of the reasons for the KMT loss, the growing closeness to China at the perceived expense of Taiwan's interests was certainly a big one. A proposed economic agreement that the government sought to railroad through the national legislature – that set off the student-led Sunflower movement of March-April 2014 – did not endear Ma to voters either. Adding to the worries of ordinary Taiwanese was Beijing's apparent breaking of its promises to Hong Kong on the 'one country, two systems' formula that in fact had originally been conceived under Deng Xiaoping as a formula for Taiwan's reunification with China.

With elections to the Taiwanese presidency and to the Legislative Yuan due in 2016, the KMT's 2014 losses surely played some role in the calculations around the Ma-Xi Jinping meeting in Singapore a year later on 7 November 2015. In the event, this was of scant help to the KMT and in January 2016, the DPP returned to the presidency with Tsai Ing-wen and also won for the first time a full majority in the Legislative Yuan.

The return of the DPP to power does not entirely resolve, however, the ambiguity in Taiwanese society about the larger relationship with the mainland. China's rapid and continuing economic growth and the close linkages between the two economies are crucial to Taiwan's own development and progress. Taiwan's distinct political development and identity formation, however, also mean that China's ideas of reunification have little traction in Taiwanese society. That said, history and ethnic ties are not easily swept aside either. In fact, more than these factors, it is perhaps a very realistic calculation that independence would invite violent reaction from the mainland, that keeps the Taiwanese sober and realistic. Even the formally pro-independence DPP has come a long way from the days of the aggressively pro-independence Chen Shui-bian.

It is these aspects of the Sino-Taiwanese relationship that many Indian commentators miss or ignore in their prescriptions to the Indian government on Taiwan policy, including calls for New Delhi to consider and engage with Taiwan in the same manner that the China-Pakistan relationship operates.

Prospects for India-Taiwan Ties

The symbolism of the Indian Prime Minister Narendra Modi's invitation to the TECC Representative to attend his swearing-in ceremony in May 2014 is important. That invitation was both an acknowledgement of gradually increasing contacts between the two sides in recent years and signified still greater interest in developing the relationship in the days ahead. Nevertheless, these contacts in the official realm are still extremely limited, when there is substantially more that could be done, besides the sporadic contacts between a few think-tanks.

The number of academic scholarships between the two sides has remained low and is mostly supported by Taiwanese institutions. Also, they are disproportionately awarded to students in the sciences. Far fewer opportunities are available for Indians interested in the Chinese language or in the social sciences. A skewed equation in favour of just the sciences ultimately does little to increase understanding between the two sides in the political, security and cultural realms – scientists generally communicate in English and remain largely apolitical. If the Taiwanese government or its institutions think that they are gaining political capital with New Delhi by disbursing science scholarships, they are mistaken. Those Indians genuinely aware of and deeply interested in Taiwan would come from the humanities and social sciences streams. These are the segments that remain largely ignored or undervalued by Taiwan's diplomatic strategists.

What is more, under the KMT regime, perhaps because of Taiwan's economic difficulties, scholarships and support for Chinese language studies for Indian students came down substantially. This in effect displayed either a lack of political foresight about the potential India offered or the belief that maintaining a stable relationship with China was Taiwan's overriding necessity that would not be alleviated by diversifying and deepening ties with other countries. However, this is a crucial area of investment if Taiwan is to have a long-term hope of support from India for greater international space. Greater knowledge and understanding of Taiwan in India that comes from student and youth exchanges are imperative for any sustainable relationship, including the development of economic relations.

Meanwhile, some progress has been achieved at least from a logistical or bureaucratic point of view in India-China relations with the decision in India by the Association of Indian Universities to recognise degrees granted in Taiwan.

People-to-people contacts meanwhile remain limited – Indian immigration officials till even a decade ago often had trouble distinguishing between the Republic of China in Taiwan and the People's Republic of China. There is rather more knowledge of Taiwan within academic institutions and think-tanks in India, particularly those based in Delhi, as scholarly exchanges and conferences on Taiwan-related themes have increased over the years. Buddhism also is a factor that increases India's importance for ordinary Taiwanese otherwise put off by impressions of a general sense of chaos and lack of safety in India. As a result, tourists from Taiwan do make their way to India and the process is made easier still with the extension of the visa-on-arrival facility to Taiwanese citizens in addition to those from China, Hong Kong and Macau.[8]

Moving on to issues specifically related to the political and economic domains, there are hardly any substantive interactions between India and Taiwan. While there is some level of unofficial military exchanges, as already mentioned, the Taiwanese are also engaged sporadically and in limited numbers at the Track 1.5 level and below, as for example, in the form of invitations to Taiwanese scholars to IDSA's annual Asian Security Conference.

On the economic side, too, there is a political reality that Indian actors need to understand, especially in the wake of the victory of the DPP in the 2014 local elections. The DPP's mayors as well as its legislators understand that the prosperity of their cities and country remains closely tied to the mainland and are unlikely to push for radical new measures asserting Taiwanese independence in international forums. What is more likely is a go-slow or a more careful negotiation over the terms of new economic agreements with China. If the DPP is serious about alternatives to China, then this will be proven only by how actively its mayors court economic investment from and opportunities for their entrepreneurs in other countries in Asia.

This is where India might need to take a leaf out of the Chinese playbook. China has long allowed its provinces and cities an extraordinary degree of freedom to engage with foreign countries and to develop partnerships with provinces and cities in other countries. Indeed, they have actively courted Taiwanese investments. China has hundreds of such sister-city and sister-province relationships across the world, including in countries that both the government and ordinary Chinese consider as potential adversaries, namely, Japan and the United States. These partnerships are a source of foreign investments, technology transfers, and people-to-people exchanges, including tourism.

India and China have already inked some such agreements between major cities and provinces. But with DPP city governments seeking to diversify their economies away from China, Indian city mayors should be courting the Taiwanese alongside other East Asians. The Indian Prime Minister's call for smart cities will also be well served by the focus on Taiwanese cities with their well-managed and technology-enabled city administration and infrastructure. This will require of India, first and foremost, the devolution of greater power in foreign policy issues to local governments in addition, of course, of Indian city mayors also gaining greater powers of administration over their own bailiwicks. At the same time, it is imperative that there is not just a national but a state- and city-level focus in India on the attainment of Chinese and other East Asian language skills as well as knowledge of the international dynamics of the region. India's candidates for the 'smart city' tag will also need to engage in smart international politics and planning.

Meanwhile, the India-Taiwan economic relationship is far from achieving its true potential. Between April 2000 and December 2015, Taiwan's FDI stock in India stood at just over (US)$165 million, accounting for just 0.6 per cent of total inflows into India in that period[9] despite possessing a foreign exchange reserve of $419 billion as of September 2014.[10] And while great hopes are being pinned on Foxconn's planned $5 billion investment in Maharashtra in the 2015-2020 period, the Taiwanese strength is in small and medium enterprises, precisely the sector that is capable of providing mass employment in India across a range of skill-sets. Of course, it cannot hurt if the Foxconn investment fructifies and is seen as succeeding, since it would then provide a major fillip to Taiwanese business interest in India. India will therefore need to focus on both prongs of the economic partnership with Taiwan.

The Taiwanese also have substantial and longstanding expertise in physical infrastructure development. In a context when China's 'one belt, one road' infrastructure investment and development initiative is the talk of Asia, and the official Indian establishment remains deeply suspicious of the Chinese plan, it might be useful for New Delhi to include Taiwanese companies in its basket of alternatives and encourage them to take up big-ticket projects in various parts of India.

What is evident from the Singapore meeting of Ma Ying-jeou and Xi Jinping is the immense ability for risk-taking and creativity that the Chinese leader displayed in meeting Ma on the eve of the elections in Taiwan. Despite the many struggles he is engaged with at home, notably the anti-corruption campaign and the downturn in China's economy, Xi managed to begin yet another important initiative. This, like the others, is no doubt equally debated and contested in the echelons of the CPC. What is more, Taiwan is a sensitive issue of considerable political and historical weight and one which also creates potential challenges to the legitimacy of the CPC and the PRC. This provides opportunities for not just the PRC's foreign rivals to exploit the situation but is also a slippery slope for Xi domestically.

From the Indian perspective, however, this Chinese move should be both an inspiration and a prod to a greater proactive approach on Taiwan.

Conclusion

India is a huge market and offers prospects similar to what China once offered for both Taiwan's large corporations as well as its small and medium enterprises. However, the same problems that are likely to afflict Tsai's attempts to turn the Taiwanese economy around and away from China might also affect her 'southward policy', which aims at building deeper engagement with South-East Asia and India, among others. The language and cultural barriers to operating in India are pretty substantial for Taiwanese businessmen. India in its turn has hitherto followed a rather inflexible version of the one-China policy compared with many other nations in East Asia and in the West. Symbolic moves by India notwithstanding, progress on the bilateral economic front has been slow, while contacts even at the functional level between government ministries and departments are intermittent and limited. There is, thus, a case to be made for greater political intervention and interactions in order to promote India-Taiwan relations.

Given that India and Taiwan are both democracies there is much that the two countries could do together. During the May 2014 general elections in India, some 100 Chinese students came visiting to observe the process.[11] How many Taiwanese delegations come visiting during various elections in India? While India and Taiwan have different electoral systems, there must surely be other lessons or insights of operating a democracy that the two sides can share. This then adds another item to the list of opportunities in which India and Taiwan have to engage with each other. For India, President-elect Tsai's 'message to the international community...that democracy, as a value, is deeply engrained in the Taiwanese people'[12] must give cause to find ways of greater engagement with the island nation on that basis.

There is also a case to be built up for greater people-to-people exchanges as well as greater institutional cooperation between universities, research institutions, think-tanks and local governments in India and Taiwan. Given the depth and breadth of China's own contacts with Taiwan and given how important Asian and Western countries interact with Taiwan, there remains little logic for the Indian government to continue with its snail's pace on pushing forward greater engagement with Taiwan. Even if

Taiwanese political leaders in government might be kept at arm's length, there is no cause to hesitate or go slow on functional cooperation at all levels of government and between all manner of institutions on the two sides.

NOTES

1. Sean Mclain, 'Foxconn plans to spend $5 billion on factories in India's Maharashtra state', *Wall Street Journal.* 8 August 2015, http://www.wsj.com/articles/foxconn-plans-to-spend-5-billion-on-factories-in-indias-maharashtra-state-1439035640
2. Ministry of External Affairs, India, 'Transcript of External Affairs Minister's first formal interaction with the media (September 8, 2014)', http://mea.gov.in/media-briefings.htm?dtl/23982/Transcript+of+External+Affairs+Ministers+first+formal+interaction+with+the+media+September+8+2014
3. On the same subject, see also Prashant Kumar Singh, 'The "One-India policy" needs more thought', *The Diplomat*, 5 November 2014, http://thediplomat.com/2014/11/the-one-india-policy-needs-more-thought/
4. Elvis Picardo, '10 countries with the biggest forex reserves', *Investopedia*, 31 March 2015, http://www.investopedia.com/articles/investing/033115/10-countries-biggest-forex-reserves.asp
5. See, for instance, Yimou Lee, 'Shadowy Chinese agency woos Taiwanese to win island back', *Japan Times,* 27 November 2014, http://www.japantimes.co.jp/news/2014/11/27/world/politics-diplomacy-world/chinas-shadowy-agency-working-swallow-taiwan/
6. Lee would subsequently be expelled from the KMT for founding the pro-independence Taiwan Solidarity Union.
7. Wen-Ti Sung, 'The rise of the "Pan-DPP 6.88": Leveling the playing field', *Thinking Taiwan*, 30 November 2014, http://thinking-taiwan.com/the-rise-of-the-pan-dpp-6-88-leveling-the-playing-field/
8. Ministry of Home Affairs, Government of India, 2016, 'e-Tourist Visa', http://indianvisaonline.gov.in/visa/tvoa.html
9. Department of Industrial Policy & Promotion, Ministry of Commerce & Industry, Government of India, 2015. 'Quarterly fact sheet: fact sheet on foreign direct investment (FDI) From April, 2000 To December, 2015', http://dipp.nic.in/English/Publications/FDI_Statistics/2015/FDI_FactSheet_OctoberNovemberDecember2015.pdf
10. Picardo, '10 countries with the biggest forex reserves', n. 4.
11. *Indian Express,* 'Chinese youth to take part in Election Commission rally today', 9 November 2013, http://www.indianexpress.com/news/chinese-youth-to-take-part-in-election-commission-rally-today/1192726/
12. Democratic Progressive Party, Taiwan, 'President-elect Tsai Ing-Wen calls for unity following election, Remarks from the International Press Conference' *Taiwan Democratic Progressive Party Mission in the U.S.,* 16 January 2016. http://us7.campaign-archive2.com/?u=514c164469699ac1ac10bfe93&id=d75de0c99b&e=b579d6a0a4

5

India and Taiwan: Two Democracies and Two Governing Systems—A View from India

Ritu Agarwal

India and Taiwan have inherited different political institutions, ideas and political personalities which have dominated the two countries over the years, but both have established the democratic political system. India has a long history of vibrant electoral democracy while Taiwan has recently chosen the path of presidential elections. Still, the larger question is why Indian democracy remains a puzzle for those who support democratic values. Political instability is often associated with democracy in India. The failure to achieve absolute majority in parliament, the multi-party system, lack of coordination between the central and state governments, and failure in achieving policy consensus are most often cited as the reasons for this trend of political uncertainty. Taiwanese democratic experience is on the other hand associated with political stability, policy consensus over matters of important political and economic issues and often much better distribution of benefits across large sections of the citizens.

This paper examines the factors which have made these two democratic countries diverge in their democratic experiences. Is the nature of the state a factor in this? How do different political institutions and their functioning influence their effectiveness? What are the factors that determine policy formulation in the two countries? How far do political ideology or economic pragmatism influence their policymaking process?

Taiwan has witnessed a changeover from an authoritarian setup to a liberal democratic political system. What factors have made this shift possible? To understand this, one has to keep in mind three factors like state capacity, rule of law and democratic institutions. In Taiwan, neither rule of law nor multiparty electoral system had been established. However, there was a developmental state supported by a strong bureaucracy. Some scholars have argued that it was the focus on economic growth which made this transition peaceful. Economic development has brought about a social transformation and desire for modernity and secular values, which have made democracy possible in Taiwan. Social transformation can be understood in terms of discarding traditional values of old loyalties, be it with the village, community or the lineage; rather, one gets more affiliated with modern ideas. This works more towards gaining one's identity as a member of a secular agency. Citizenship as a modern concept becomes more important, which can be defined as membership of a state organisation. People do not organise themselves around the traditional social institutions; rather, they get membership of the political associations of civic bodies. This kind of social transformation has given hope for modernity. Social mobility has become an essential feature and it has bridged the gap between rich and poor and thus flattened social hierarchies in significant ways. These social conditions play a significant role in democratic consolidation in a country.

India is a very different model of democracy, where economic growth has not brought much social transformation. Its literacy rate remains unsatisfactory, and its people are mostly organised around the traditional social institutions like caste, religion and community. In India, one's identity is determined by the place and the family in which one is born. These traditional loyalties bind people and their life throughout. The lack of social mobilisation has not created enough conditions for modernity in India. Social hierarchies play a significant role and are not conducive to a successful democratic political system. Even the state is not able to penetrate deep into these social boundaries, which restrict individual freedom and personal rights. Thus the state's capacity is negotiated and constrained by social norms and traditional institutions. State control, often with the rule of law and multiparty electoral system, fails to deliver social goods and society fails to work as complementary to the state's goals and objectives.

In Taiwan, the traditional Confucian culture works as a supporting mechanism in many ways. Confucianism inculcates respect for the elders, faith in the political empire and obedience to its command. Culturally, people are accustomed to following orders and carrying out the social agendas set for them. Confucianism, which was historically considered an impediment to modernisation, has actually worked to create social harmony and cooperation and thus attenuated social conflicts. The state prioritises the developmental agenda from above, which is followed by the local and regional players at the grassroots level. In India, on the other hand, different kinds of group and community interests sometimes override the larger state and national interests. There is no inclination to follow political orders from above; rather, the political ideas are always contested and their implementation is questioned. These factors have made India more conflict prone and divided along group and community interests. Even the electoral politics caters to these different regional and community interests, which makes this scenario more competitive and contested. The social forces are more independent in nature and most often work as autonomous actors in fulfilling the local and regional interest. The lack of political stability and poor coordination between the national and local interests leads to India being regarded as a weak state.

To understand the nature of democracy in Taiwan and India, it is also important to examine the role of political institutions like the Constitution, law and the state. How does the regime gain political legitimacy? Is it based on a purely institutional model of governance or are there different mechanisms to gain popular legitimacy in these two countries?

Economic performance is the key to attaining political legitimacy in countries which earlier have been authoritarian. The state has played quite an active role in promoting market forces in Taiwan, which has been the main factor behind its economic miracle. The most important initiative in this direction has been the implementation of land reform. Under this programme, the farmers were granted more freedom in making economic decisions. Even as early as 1950, in industries, the share of the private sector was much larger than that of the government. The government induced privatisation of the economy and the mushrooming of small-scale family businesses played a crucial role in the economic boom of the country. Another important feature of state-induced privatisation has been the increase in foreign capital investment. The high domestic saving rate and impressive amount of foreign investment have led to large-scale capital accumulation. This capital was used mainly for infrastructure development. State planning was mainly towards building up the growth and economic structure with less regulation. Thus, the state and capital have worked together to bring about economic growth, which in a way has gained political legitimacy for the regime.

In India, the large population, traditional beliefs and protecting cultural values have been more on the forefront of the agenda of political parties. Political development is not necessarily associated with the distribution of economic goods. The state in India has never been regarded as developmental in nature. Political participation has not brought about social mobilisation, and the polity is often divided along caste, class and religious lines. Ideas like secularism, affirmative action and preferential policies are regularly contested politically. The bureaucracy also is embedded in the dominant social and economic interests. The state is not an autonomous actor which can decide on the stage of economic development India should attain, the kind of industrial growth that is beneficial and how the economic benefits should be distributed equitably. While equality and justice are the two dominant ideologies which have generated considerable debate in the academia and among policymakers, the lack of social reforms and progressive state interventions has made the Indian state incapable of performing its social and economic functions. India has mainly remained a primordial society where the traditional identities and social bondages play a dominant role. An agrarian economy, it suffers from unequal land distribution, farmers' debt and often the dominant role of middlemen in marketing strategies. Though the state has taken a few pro-active measures, the implementation part is determined by local-level leaders and their vision about their regions.

An interesting feature of the Taiwanese economic miracle is the great adaptability of the system to changing circumstances. In a period when inflation was a major problem, the whole effort was focused on reducing inflation and promoting industrialisation. Initially, the emphasis was on building up labour-intensive industries. The shift from labour- to capital- to knowledge-based industries was very much planned and was adopted according to the changing circumstances.

The Indian state has not been farsighted enough to lay down the objectives for economic performance. Elections are the key parameters to test the political legitimacy of a particular party. There is not a single and consistent approach towards the national objectives. With elections deciding the fate of a political party, there is a change in the national goals and objectives every time a different party comes to power. Most of the time, the parties do not bring about any structural transformation; rather, the policies are drawn towards maintaining the political status quo. Religion, caste and community often turn into great reserves to capture votes during the elections. Any economic objective which disturbs the social fabric is often not contested. To pass any legislation on crucial social and economic issues, there has to be a debate in Parliament, which itself is dominated by multiple parties and their different ideologies. One example is the land legislation law which the current government at the centre has been trying to get passed for the last two years. However, it has been unable to gain the consent in the upper house of Parliament. This has become a major block in attracting foreign investment into the country.

Taiwan has evolved a political system which has features of the unitary model but there was some tendency to become centralised. Taiwan does not give supremacy to any political institution like the executive over the legislature; rather, it has devolved political power to the local government to take initiatives. Local innovations play an important role in evolving new policy objectives. Constitutionally, there are five branches of government, including the executive, the legislative and the judiciary, and in addition two more political organs, which are responsible for the recruitment and monitoring of these officials. Since Taiwan started its journey of democratisation quite late, there is a view among scholars that civil and political rights are not granted fully to its citizens. In fact, the language of political protest and dissent seems to be different in the country. However, the citizens have been granted more religious freedom. There is also much more social freedom of association and movement. In India, there is most often no clear separation of powers and there is an institutional overlap, which makes decision-making difficult. Protracted debates on legislative matters further delay the political process. Besides, there are political agitations. Lobbies and pressure groups also influence political decision-making.

Law and order is crucial to provide confidence to foreign investment. Laws create favourable conditions and provide guidelines about the areas in which economic investment can be made. In India, the rule of law plays the role as a supervisor and maintains law and order. The law in Taiwan manly works as a tool of the state to provide the conditions which can become a structural ground for the capitalist economic interest. It mainly deals with social and economic rights and is silent about civil and political rights.

In India, law and legal freedom are quite powerful instruments in the hands of the state. These mainly work to serve the political interest of a community or a group. The laws are mainly concerned with social and political issues and do not address economic freedom and investment. A plethora of legislation has been passed in the country over the decades, but there is little clarity in them. Often, the laws seem to be not related to the prevailing social reality. The judiciary has taken an active role of social intervention and public interest litigation gives the right to the citizens to fight against corruption, public policy and other political process. However, there is evidence of high-level authorities not adhering to judicial orders if the person to be proceeded against is influential. Often, the judicial system is also used vindictively.

Sun Yat Sen's Three People's Principles (nationalism, democracy and livelihood) seem to dominate the official political ideology in Taiwan. The very idea of establishing a link between political and economic development fits into the country's development trajectory. Economic growth was considered the key to bring social modernisation, which would lead to democracy eventually. This was well reflected in the early ideological debates in Taiwan, when free market and free trade were important tenets of economic development. However, there were no alternative ideologies suggested and the political culture seems to be more pragmatic in nature. In India, Nehru's vision of a strong and economically developed country has often led to political contestation. There is not a single dominating political vision.

In Taiwan, the success of democratisation is also based on the party system, which for several years was dominated by a one-party system. The party was economically very powerful and controlled most of the economic and political positions. However, after the 1970s, Taiwan witnessed the emergence of opposition parties. There is, currently, mainly a two-party system, which has made government functioning quite effective. The multi-party system in India, based on different political ideologies, often makes governance much more difficult.

In Taiwan, the democratic consolidation seems to be happening due to the forces from below. Though there is a unitary model of political governance, the local political institutions have been given a more free hand in taking economic initiatives at various levels. This has not only brought social change but also satisfied large sections of society. In India, the local politics fail to evolve an innovative model of governance which satisfies the larger sections of society. Due to the federal structure of government, the party at the centre cannot dictate the terms of development to the states. However, in recent years Bihar and some southern states have become popular in evolving a focused approach to development.

In India's democratic experience, there is a diversity of political interest, which is most often accompanied by a deliberative and consultative political process. There is a complex process of interest articulation in this multicultural society. The political situation can be described as democratic management of contentious politics. Taiwan on the other hand has been a vibrant young democracy marked by linguistic and religious homogeneity. Democracy in Taiwan has been shaped by Confucian traditions, social harmony and Western liberalism.

The political process in India is one of maintaining elusive consensus driven by competing interest articulation. But there is an institutional deficit for accommodating these diverse social interests. In Taiwan, there has been a political consensus on the larger national interest. Policies are formulated according to the national requirement and the country seems to be having a greater institutional capacity which can better coordinate between the government and the citizens.

In Taiwan, there has been minimal popular opposition to government, including to some of the reforms. The Confucian values of duty and piety may have played a role in this. Moreover, lower levels of inequality have allowed the government to implement reforms with little resistance. There has been pragmatism in policymaking accompanied by continuity in policy formulation. Moreover, policies are formulated according to the need of the time. The regimes have shown their ability to identify the needs and devise and implement national development programmes on the basis of requirement rather than prevalent ideologies. Policy formulation is based on trial and error. Policies are oriented towards local development and adopt a political approach suited to local conditions. In India, as we have seen earlier, there is a problem of policy continuity.

The Taiwanese state can be defined as an entrepreneurial state tilted towards building a market-based economy, thus resolving efforts to bring about material well-being. The state has also been playing an active role in promoting export-led growth and establishing an industrial economy. The Indian state on the other hand is more involved in policy formulation but not in making active interventions in industrial promotion. In India there is a separation of powers, clearly laid down by the constitution, and there has been no coordination between ministries and industrial groups. There are various forums which often provide a contradictory picture about the ground reality.

Thus, there is a huge difference in the historical and political situation in which democracy has evolved in India and Taiwan. In India, with its multiple diversity of interests, often not the political consent but the contestation is regarded as a viable alternative to make democracy successful as a political process. It also brings down the role that political institutions can play in democratic management of the country. Taiwan's experience on the other hand points out the ideal model of democracy where social forces and political institutions work in harmony.

6

India and Taiwan: Potential Regional Partners?

Jagannath P. Panda

The significance of India and Taiwan, as two prominent economies of Asia, is ever increasing. India is one of the largest economies in the world, whereas Taiwan is one of the most competitive economies in the Asia-Pacific region.[1] While Taiwan is known for its export and investment policy in Asia-Pacific, India is a vital economy in the Regional Comprehensive Economic Partnership (RCEP) negotiation mechanism, which is one of the most important trade liberalising models of the region. The two countries' 'complex' relationship with the People's Republic of China (PRC) gives them further prominence.

Is there scope for cooperation between India and Taiwan in Asia-Pacific or in the evolving regional order? In 2015 the two countries commemorated the 20th anniversary of the establishment of the India-Taipei Association (ITA) in Taipei and the Taipei Economic and Cultural Center (TECC) in New Delhi. These representative offices have allowed them to maintain a working relation which is not diplomatic but comprises diplomatic shades. This chapter argues that diplomacy has many characters and gradations, and therefore, there is scope for India and Taiwan to cooperate in the evolving regional order. For this, Taiwan has to carefully prepare a path for itself in the regional order to seek India's support whereas India has also equally to take an interest to cooperate with Taiwan. The scope of this cooperation is more in multilateral forums, mechanisms and institutions by supporting each other's position and participation. Both countries need to think ambitiously, not ambiguously, for a greater role and participation in the regional mechanisms and multilateral institutions in an evolving regional order where the focus is on Indo-Pacific.

Between Asia-Pacific Ambitions and Ambiguity

Three conditions prompt India and Taiwan to ponder a channel of cooperation by supporting each other's position and participation in regional mechanisms and institutions. *First*, they need each other to enhance their international space and role. Experts argue that 'international space is mostly construed for partaking in multilateral institutions and mechanisms, be they diplomatic or non-diplomatic, official or non-official, political or economic'.[2] Taiwan has been constantly looking to enhance its international space, through membership and participation in regional and global institutions or bodies, since the 1990s,[3] not only in terms of getting affiliation in United Nations affiliated bodies but also to get accession to trading mechanisms and financial institutions. From 1993 onwards, Taiwan has annually attempted to persuade the UN General Assembly to include in its agenda the deliberation of the issue of UN representation for its 23 million people. The Ma Ying-jeou administration in its first term advocated for greater space for Taiwan in international agencies through 'meaningful participation'.[4] For instance, on 14 August 2008, Taiwan with the cooperation of 16 diplomatic allies submitted a proposal to the UN Secretariat for 'meaningful participation in international agencies' affiliated to the UN, which was rejected. For Taipei, 'meaningful participation' denotes 'autonomy to decide when and what activities it wishes to join at the global level, instead of relying on the mainland'.[5] In its second term, the Ma Ying-jeou administration attempted to promote Taiwan's case for greater international participation in the Asia-Pacific region. The newly elected Democratic Progressive Party (DPP) may also follow a similar path. Likewise, partaking in multilateral forums and mechanisms has been a frequently debated topic in Indian foreign policy in recent times. Under Prime Minister Narendra Modi, Indian foreign policy is witnessing a new lease of progress where the aim is to enhance India's positioning in global platforms. Experts argue that 'Modi has certainly aroused expectations at home and abroad about India's rise in the global scene in the 21st century with the most imaginative way and clarity of purpose'.[6] This similar quest in India's and Taiwan's foreign policy must encourage them to ponder possible cooperation.

Second, the rise of the 'Indo-Pacific' construct where the focus is on maritime security must bring India and Taiwan together. Taiwan is a key linking point for important sea-lanes in Indo-Pacific.[7] Its proximity to the South China Sea makes its strategic positioning significant. The region of South-East Asia, which possesses a substantial portion of the South China Sea zone, spans over Sumatra to Taiwan and becomes a critical maritime zone linking both the Indian and Pacific Oceans.[8] Taiwan is heavily dependent on sea trade. This must encourage India and Taiwan to come together. Given India's central positioning in the Indian Ocean and its rising commercial ambition in the South China Sea, India's maritime reach across the region must board Taiwan. On the maritime territorial sector, especially on the South China Sea issue, there may not be any practical cooperation possible between India and Taiwan since India is not a party to the South China Sea dispute. But both India and Taiwan must start thinking about maritime trade and commercial cooperation in building peace and stability across the region, especially when the then President Ma Ying-jeou's 'South China Sea Peace Initiative' appealed to the parties in dispute to put aside the differences and 'promote joint development of resources'.[9] This correlates with India's approach towards the South China Sea where exploration of resources and promoting commercial activities are India's key motives. India and Taiwan can talk about how they can promote resource exploration in Sea zone.

Third, the evolving Asia-Pacific trade architecture must also encourage India and Taiwan to search for a cooperative drive. Both sides definitely possess potential economies but their potentialities do not often place them in a comfortable economic zone in Asia-Pacific trade architecture. Establishing a free trade area (FTA) has been a much talked-about aspect of the Asia-Pacific region in recent times. There is much discussion about the Trans-Pacific Partnership (TPP) and the RCEP mechanisms. Neither Taiwan nor India is part of the TPP negotiation process. Their exclusion from the TPP must encourage them to cooperate on a positive spectrum. This becomes critical considering that Taiwan is an important part of the Asian supply chain as a key regional investor and export link.[10] To its disadvantage, Taiwan's commercial interest and importance needs to be explored in the Asia-Pacific trade models. Likewise, India's non-membership in Asia Pacific Economic Cooperation (APEC) has limited its scope to partake in the Asia-Pacific trade mechanisms. These create new conditions for India-Taiwan cooperation in the regional sphere.

Fourth, what puts India and Taiwan on a common platform is the factor of the People's Republic of China (PRC). India's relations with China are steadily improving, but the enduring strategic underpinning, especially concerning the boundary dispute, hampers their relationship. On a similar footing, under President Ma Ying-jeou, mainland China-Taiwan relations became somewhat stable and went on a progressive path on the economic front. However, overall, these relations continue to remain tense on the reunification issue and on the matter of the one-China policy. The arrival of the DPP in power in Taiwan has brought this one-China policy in the reckoning again. Though both India and Taiwan may find it difficult to pursue an anti-China (for India) or anti-mainland (for Taiwan) foreign policy, a cooperative context of understanding on China's rise in Asia can be a bonding factor between them. This is important, given that China under Xi Jinping has become a demanding power and has been pursuing an 'assertive' policy both regionally and globally.

New Institutions and Trade Architecture

Even though the regional order is in flux currently, still it offers India and Taiwan greater scope for cooperation than ever before. The scope to cooperate at the regional level is more vividly observed in regional mechanisms and multilateral institutions than anywhere else. Greater participation in the multilateral forums and institutions has been one of the main pillars of Taiwan's identity in the international sphere. Similarly, for India, a greater role in regional mechanisms and institutions would enhance its status as a power both in Asia and beyond. A serious deliberation for cooperation between the two sides on a set of new institutions or mechanisms must start. Given the intertwining of 'economic multilateral' mechanisms with 'security multilateral' mechanisms, India and Taiwan can forge dialogue on a range of issues like the Asian Infrastructural Investment Bank (AIIB), RCEP, TPP and the FTA of Asia-Pacific (FTAAP).

The AIIB, which is a newly established financial institution, should encourage India and Taiwan to envision regional cooperation. *Can India and Taiwan practically cooperate within the sphere of the AIIB, given that it is a Chinese-propounded institution*? Taiwan applied for AIIB founding membership at the beginning of 2015, but China prevented the application, explaining that Taiwan can apply later after consultation with mainland China with an 'appropriate name'. Nomenclature is a sensitive issue between Taiwan and mainland China. Jin Liqun, president of the AIIB, expressed the view that Taiwan's proposal for membership must come through the Finance Ministry of the PRC, to which Taiwan may not agree.[11] Article 3 of Chapter I of the AIIB restricts entry to 'sovereign' countries.[12] Taiwan on its part wants to be a part of the AIIB on terms of 'dignity and equality'.[13] But seen from a practical perspective, Taiwan may compromise on the nomenclature of its name in order to join the AIIB. In this context, it may be noted that Taiwan has enhanced its international participation through names like 'Chinese Taipei', 'Taipei, China' and 'Separate Customs Territory of Taiwan, Penghu, Kinmen and Matsu'. Inclusion in the AIIB will allow Taiwan to cooperate with a range of regional and non-regional countries economically.

Taiwan's entry into the AIIB is possible under the name of 'Taipei, China', similar to the name that Taiwan holds in the Asian Development Bank (ADB); or under the Hong Kong model, under which Taiwan has to apply through China's Finance Ministry; or the APEC model, where Taiwan can be inducted as 'Chinese Taipei' as an 'official member', with the same rights and obligations as other members enjoy. Given Taiwan's possible entry into the AIIB, a range of scope for cooperation may be crafted between India and Taiwan. India as the second-largest shareholder in the AIIB can ideally support Taiwan's entry. For India, it may be difficult to support Taiwan's bid outright, but with a tactical understanding between the two sides it may be possible. Taiwan's entry into the AIIB would allow the two countries to cooperate on a range of regional economic issues and forge discussion on regional economic integration, where the focus should be on infrastructural development. The two sides can cooperate in areas like energy, transport, logistics, rural development, urban development, education, healthcare, and social development.

On a broader spectrum, this ambition of cooperation should not be limited to the AIIB. Asia-Pacific is undergoing transition currently and the highlight is the emerging trade architecture. Negotiations of the TPP have been concluded; the RCEP negotiations are ongoing. Collaboration on these trade negotiating models can be a medium of cooperation between India and Taiwan. Taiwan's Economic Cooperation Framework Agreement (ECFA) with mainland China has allowed it to forge an understanding with many countries to sign FTA-like agreements. Not being a sovereign entity, Taipei cannot generally sign full-fledged FTAs,[14] but it has signed FTA-like agreements with New Zealand and Singapore. Taiwan's FTA-like agreement with New Zealand has been conducted under the New Zealand and the Separate Customs Territory of Taiwan, Penghu, Kinmen, and Matsu on Economic Cooperation (ANZTEC). This agreement was signed in July 2013. ANZTEC is a high-quality comprehensive trade agreement that will promote trade in goods, services and investments.[15] It would also offer preferential tariff access to New Zealand exporters in Taiwan.[16] Singapore is the first South-East Asian country with whom Taiwan entered into an FTA-like agreement, on a pattern similar to ANZTEC, in November 2013. It is formally known as the Agreement between Singapore and the Separate Customs Territory of Taiwan, Penghu, Kinmen and Matsu on Economic Partnership (ASTEP),[17] which is described as a 'high-standard' and 'high-quality' trade agreement.[18] ANZTEC and ASTEP are two milestones in Taiwan's progress in regional participation and regional economic integration, especially when Singapore is a part of the RCEP negotiation model and New Zealand is already a part of the TPP.

An FTA-like agreement between India and Taiwan is being discussed for sometime now and a feasibility study has been conducted by the Indian

Council for Research on International Economic Relations (ICRIER) and the Chung-Hua Institution for Economic Research. Experts state that an FTA-like agreement between India and Taiwan will yield mutual benefits, promote further economic exchange and bring about high complementarities in trade and industrial structure.[19] Eliminating tariff and non-tariff barriers, the agreement will enhance trade and investment ties.[20] This will also result in more Taiwanese investment in India and Indian firms will be more attracted to collaborate with the Taiwanese firms. But there is a hitch. Since India does not have an FTA with China, Beijing may express its concern over an India-Taiwan FTA-like agreement. The challenge for India and Taiwan is to craft diligently an FTA-like agreement that will seem non-official, and mostly look like a non-governmental understanding between the two sides.

The current trade volume between India and Taiwan is not impressive. By 2014, their bilateral trade was around (US) $6 billion. In 1995, the year when the representative offices were established on both sides, the trade figure was merely around $934 million.[21] There has been a growth since then but the trade contacts do not match the potential. Given India's concern with China over trade imbalance, India can learn from Taiwan how to address the trade imbalance since Taiwan maintains a trade surplus (as per the 2014 statistics) with mainland China.[22]

The ambition to become a part of the TPP and the regional trade architecture must draw India and Taiwan closer. Neither India nor Taiwan is a part of the TPP currently. India has not been invited to join the TPP primarily for two reasons. India is not a member of APEC; and the Indian economy is not well-integrated into the Pacific countries' economies. Taiwan would like to become a part of the TPP, even when mainland China is not a part of it. Endorsement of key APEC members who are part of the TPP will be crucial in Taiwan's quest for TPP membership. China, as a member of APEC may object, but Taiwan can bank upon the support of the United States and other APEC economies to help make it to the TPP. Five of Taiwan's top 10 export partners are TPP economies.[23] Taiwan argues that TPP inclusion for itself will create a pathway for the Chinese-proposed FTA of Asia-Pacific (FTAAP) since the eventual purpose of these trade liberalizing models is regional integration.[24]

Meanwhile, India's scope for a possible membership in APEC is rising.[25] There is a growing chorus emerging in favour of India's possible membership in APEC. India's tryst with APEC has been a two-decades-long struggle so far. In 1997, India was not inducted when the issue of inducting new members in APEC was in its prime debate. India repeated its membership request in 2007, which is still pending. APEC membership requires a consensus on the application by all members. India was mainly denied APEC admission on the ground that its economy was not integrated into the global system and India was unable to gain confidence among APEC members. It has been further argued that with frequent government changes in India in the late 1990s, the coalition governments did not pursue the matter seriously. In later years, there was a membership freeze within APEC.

Currently, India's chance of APEC membership has amplified substantially. The new Indian government aims to carry forward trade, investment and infrastructure development as its major goals. In the last few years, despite slow growth, the Indian economy has become more translucent, open and free for trade and investment, which is one of the main goals of APEC.[26] Besides, India's economic ties with APEC members have been growing. In addition, India's Look East policy (now Act East policy) has become more institutionalised, where it has gained more conviction as an economic power among the key APEC members. With Singapore, Thailand, Indonesia, and Malaysia, India today is engaged more deliberately bilaterally as well as institutionally through ASEAN, the East Asia Summit (EAS) and through the ongoing negotiation of the RCEP mechanisms. India's engagement with the US and Japan, the two leading economies, has deepened economically and strategically. India has participated in RCEP negotiations since the beginning and has shown a lot of promise for economic integration at the regional level. Besides, India's engagements with regional and global economic regimes have also improved, where the country is known as a promising developing economy as a BRICS member. India's quest for APEC membership may therefore be only a question of when. Given this, India and Taiwan must explore possible opportunities on how to cooperate in these emerging Asia-Pacific architectures.

Taiwan's entry into APEC was possible under 'separate economy'. For APEC membership, a prospective member must be a 'separate economy' and not necessarily a 'separate state'. In fact, APEC members are known as member economies rather than member countries. Under the name of 'Chinese Taipei', Taiwan made it to APEC in November 1991. In the same year, the PRC also made it to APEC as a member along with Hong Kong. Hong Kong, now a Special Administrative Region of the PRC, entered APEC as a 'British Colony'. India was invited to attend the APEC meeting as an observer in November 2011. Since Taiwan is already a member of APEC, it can be helpful in generating support for India. India needs China's support along with that of the US and Japan to win consensus in its favour for APEC entry. 'Chinese Taipei's' open support in this regard will be crucial.

Besides, the merits and significance of RCEP must also be contemplated in India-Taiwan relations. From the outset, India has supported the idea of RCEP and has participated in launching the RCEP negotiation process. India has shown keen interest in joining RCEP though it is still hesitant about an FTA with China, and there are worries that Chinese goods may flood the Indian market through RCEP. Overall, ASEAN's significance in Indian foreign policy makes New Delhi take the RCEP negotiation seriously. RCEP would not only facilitate India's greater presence in the South-East or East Asian market; it will also facilitate India's Act East policy massively in economic dealings. Not only does India share an FTA with ASEAN but also with two of the main dialogue partners of ASEAN – Japan and South Korea. RCEP will provide a substantial platform for India to maximise its trade profile and economic, services and communications contacts with the ASEAN communities, which will lead to greater cooperation in areas like banking, tourism and societal interactions.[27] Above all this, partaking in RCEP will enhance India's Asia-Pacific undertaking. Taiwan must take these aspects seriously. Taiwan does not have an FTA with ASEAN but it has an FTA-like agreement with Singapore. Taiwan must aim to further sign FTA-like agreements not only with other ASEAN economies but also with the dialogue partners of the ASEAN. This will be critical since RCEP involves six dialogue partners – Australia, China, India, Japan, the Republic of Korea (RoK), and New Zealand. Taiwan's closer economic cooperation with India and other RCEP negotiating dialogue partners will be beneficial for its future.

Envisioning a Possible Convergence

Taiwan's Go South policy factors both ASEAN and India prominently.[28] The main target under this policy has been how to promote bilateral trade, agricultural and fishery cooperation with the ASEAN countries. One of the envisaged means to push forward these policy objectives has been for Taiwan to establish more representative offices in South-East Asia. With India, the main target has been how to push forward an FTA-like agreement and enhance cooperation in science &technology. The newly elected DPP looks determined to continue with Taiwan's Go South policy, where India is a vital factor.[29] India's rising profile as a progressive economy is the main reason why Taiwan factors India prominently in its Go South policy. In a broader spectrum, Taiwan's Go South policy corroborates with India's Act East policy. Even though Taiwan is not the main factor in India's Act East policy, there is a scope emerging for Taiwan and India to take note of their converging foreign policies and establish cooperation at the bilateral and regional levels. Taiwan's economy has slowed down in the last several years. Under the Kuomintang (KMT) rule, the economic slowdown continued. KMT's main intent was to follow a policy of economic engagement with China and improve the cross-Strait relations as well as Taiwan's economic condition. But that didn't really offer the intended result the KMT was aiming for. The economic slowdown in Taiwan was one of the reasons why the KMT lost the election. The DPP campaigned for a greater identity for Taiwan and advocated for greater engagement with other nations in Asia, besides China.[30] India factors in that stratagem. Thus, there is scope for convergence between India's Act East policy and Taiwan's Go South policy. Prime Minister Modi's Make in India campaign will benefit from the Taiwanese investments. Companies like Foxconn and Wistron Corp have shown interest to invest in India recently. There is a need to capitalise on and push forward this engagement.

The emerging Indo-Pacific order must also be a converging point of interaction between India and Taiwan. The then President Ma Ying-jeou stated broadly that Taiwan has three major roles to play in Asia: promoting free trade, contributing to the regional trade networks as a valuable economy, and driving the regional prosperity as an economy. The new President, Tsai Ing-Wen, also aims to promote similar ideas in Taiwan's greater regional context. Prime Minister Modi in India has also envisioned a similar role for India. He has advocated for free and fair trade in Asia, enhancing regional trade networks and maintaining Asia's prosperity through a shared leadership in the continent. In a broader spectrum, the choice before India and Taiwan is compelling to forge greater cooperation at the regional level.

NOTES

1. *The Global Competitiveness Report 2014-2015* ranks Taiwan as the 14th most important economy and among the top ten competitive economies in the Asia-Pacific region. See Thierry Geiger, 'Global Competitiveness and Risk', World Economic Forum, 2 September 2014, https://www.weforum.org/agenda/2014/09/top-10-competitive-economies-asia-pacific/ (accessed on 29 April 2016).
2. Bonnie S. Glaser, *Taiwan's Quest for Greater Participation in the International Community, A report of the CSIS Freeman Chair in China Studies*, Centre for Strategic & International Studies, Rowman & Littlefield, November 2013, p. 1.
3. Ibid.
4. See Jagannath P. Panda, 'Taiwan's Failure at the UN', *IDSA Comment,* 24 September 2008, http://www.idsa.in/idsastrategiccomments/TaiwansFailureattheUN_JPPanda_240908 (accessed on 6 May 2016).
5. Ibid.
6. P. Stobdan, 'Modi and India's Rise on World Stage', *IDSA News* (Published earlier in *The Pioneer*), 20 December 2015, http://www.idsa.in/idsanews/modi-and-indian-rise-on-world-stage_pstobdan_201215 (accessed on 6 May 2016).
7. Prakash Katoch, 'Taiwan – Why Shy Full Relations?', *Indian Defence Review,* 4 December 2015, http://www.indiandefencereview.com/news/taiwan-why-shy-full-relations/ (accessed on 6 May 2016).
8. Ji Guoxing, 'SLOC security in the Asia-Pacific', *Centre Occasional Paper,* Asia-Pacific Centre for Security, Hawaii, February 2000, http://apcss.org/Publications/Ocasional%20Papers/OPSloc.htm (accessed on 6 May 2016).
9. 'Taiwan President proposes South China Sea peace initiative', *Focus Taiwan,* 26 May 2015, http://focustaiwan.tw/news/aipl/201505260006.aspx (accessed on 6 May 2016); see also Shannon Tiezzi, 'Taiwan's plan for peace in the South China Sea', *The Diplomat,* 27 May 2015, http://thediplomat.com/2015/05/taiwans-plan-for-peace-in-the-south-china-sea/ (accessed on 28 April 2016).
10. Kevin G. Nealer and Margaux Fimbres, 'Taiwan and regional trade organizations: an urgent need for fresh ideas', *Asia Policy,* no. 21, January 2016, p. 5.
11. Yuan-Ming Chiao, 'Taiwan AIIB member bid must go through PRC ministry: China', *China Post,* 10 April 2016, http://www.chinapost.com.tw/print/463044.htm (accessed on 6 May 2016).

12. Ibid. Article 3 of the Articles of Agreement of the AIIB states that 'In the case of an applicant which is not sovereign or not responsible for the conduct of its international relations, application for membership in the Bank shall be presented or agreed by the member of the Bank responsible for its international relations'. See http://www.aiib.org/uploadfile/2015/0814/20150814022158430.pdf (accessed on 6 May 2016).
13. 'Government gives up AIIB application for "dignity"', *Taipei Times,* 13 April 2016, http://www.taipeitimes.com/News/front/print/2016/04/13/2003643828 (accessed on 6 May 2016).
14. Taiwan has FTAs with most of its diplomatic allies in Central America such as Panama, Guatemala, Nicaragua, El Salvador and Honduras.
15. 'What is ANZTEC?', New Zealand Commerce and Industry Office, Taipei, http://nzcio.com/node/249/view (accessed on 6 May 2016).
16. Ibid.
17. Shih Hsiu-chuan, 'Taiwan, Singapore sign free-trade pact', *Taipei Times*, 8 November 2013, http://www.taipeitimes.com/News/front/archives/2013/11/08/2003576388 (accessed on 6 May 2016).
18. Ibid.
19. Kristy Hsu, 'India-Taiwan economic partnership: building a new growth model', *Indian Foreign Affairs Journal,* vol. 8, no. 3, July-September 2013, p. 298.
20. Ibid.
21. Tien-Sze Fang, 'India-Taiwan relations: a comprehensive security perspective', *Swarajya,* 26 February 2016, http://swarajyamag.com/world/india-taiwan-relations-a-comprehensive-security-perspective (accessed on 6 May 2016).
22. Ibid.
23. Robert Holly, 'Taiwan looks to join giant trade deal', Midwest Centre, 20 November 2015, http://investigatemidwest.org/2015/11/20/taiwan-looks-to-join-giant-trade-deal/ (accessed on 7 May 2016).
24. Goh Sui Noi, 'Taiwan looks beyond China for growth', *Strait Times,* 16 October 2015, http://www.straitstimes.com/opinion/taiwan-looks-beyond-china-for-growth (accessed on 7 May 2016).
25. This part of the paper is drawn on the author's IDSA issue brief, *Beijing's APEC Call on India: A New Twist in India-China Power Politics*, 5 August 2014, http://www.idsa.in/issuebrief/BeijingsAPECCallonIndia_jppanda-050714#footnote21_rf3o3q3 (accessed on 7 May 2016).
26. Chris Devonshire-Ellis, 'India appeals for APEC membership', *Asia Briefing,* 6 October 2013, http://www.asiabriefing.com/news/2013/10/india-appeals-apec-membership/ (accessed on 26 July 2014); Amitendu Palit, 'Cooperation 2.0: India and APEC are getting closer', *Market Express,* 24 July 2014, http://www.marketexpress.in/2014/07/cooperation-2-0-india-and-apec-are-getting-closer.html (accessed on 26 July 2014).
27. 'Ganeshan Wignaraja: RCEP is Huge for Indian Businesses Which Should Scale Up', Surojit Gupta's Interview with Ganeshan Wignaraja (opinion), *Times of India*, February 6, 2013, at http://articles.timesofindia.indiatimes.com/2013-02-06/interviews/36765453_1_rcep-indian-businesses-regional-comprehensive-economic-partnership (Accessed May 27, 2013)
28. 'Taiwan has long followed "go south" policy: ministry', *Taipei Times,* 5 October 2015,

http://www.taipeitimes.com/News/taiwan/archives/2015/10/05/2003629318 (accessed on 7 May 2016).

29. Ibid.
30. 'Winds of change: Taiwan's shifting politics opens the door to greater Indo-Taiwanese cooperation', *Times of India* (Editorial), 18 January 2016, http://blogs.timesofindia.indiatimes.com/toi-editorials/winds-of-change-taiwans-shifting-politics-opens-the-door-to-greater-indo-taiwanese-cooperation/ (accessed on 8 May 2016).

7

India-Taiwan Economic Partnership in the Asian Era

Kristy Hsu

Taiwan is a dynamic democracy. It is also the centre of the production networks and global value chains of certain manufacturing sectors, such as electronics and ICT. In the past few years, Taiwanese companies have begun to pay attention to India's potential market and the possibility of India playing the role of an emerging 'Asian Factory'.

India adopted a Look East policy in 1991 and since then has gradually prepared for further integration into the Asian regional economy and built closer economic ties with the East Asian countries. Being an active player in the region, Taiwan has the potential to be India's strategic economic partner in building a stronger manufacturing sector in the Asian Era. India can also contribute to enhancing Taiwan's participation in the global value chains and rebalancing its economic relations with China.

Two Decades of India-Taiwan Economic Relations

The year 2015 marked the 20th anniversary of establishing India-Taiwan official relations. In March 1995, the India-Taipei Association (ITA) in Taipei and the Taipei Economic and Cultural Center (TECC) in New

Delhi were established.[1] Since then economic and trade activities and people-to-people exchanges between the two sides have been growing.

Informally, India-Taiwan economic ties grew in the 1980s. In these early years, Indian trading companies opened up subsidiaries in Taiwan and sourced consumer products from Taiwan, such as textiles and garments and electronic equipments and exported from India gold, silk and other natural resources. However, after the Taiwan government allowed direct investment in mainland China in 1992, most Indian trading companies followed Taiwanese companies to China and closed their operations in Taiwan. The retreat of the early Indian presence from Taiwan to some extent reflected the trend of Taiwan's Go West movement.

In 2003 Taiwan's Ministry of Economic Affairs decided to include India in the priority list of its trade promotion programmes. This new policy unveiled India as a market of tremendous possibilities and potential to Taiwan business sector at large. The past decade has witnessed bilateral trade growing at an average of two digits and reaching a historic high at (US)$7.57 billion in 2011 before it lost its momentum. In 2014, the trade volume continued to drop and declined to (US)$5.91 billion, accounting for around one per cent of Taiwan's external trade.[2]

Taiwan has been among the top investors in China and South-East Asia, but passive in investing in India. Compared with Japan and Korea, Taiwan is also a latecomer in India. According to the Department of Industrial Policy & Promotion (DIPP), Ministry of Commerce and Industry of India, Taiwan was ranked as the 43rd FDI source during the 2000 to September 2015 period, with accumulated FDI volume amounting to (US)$106.4 million, accounting for only 0.04 per cent of India's total FDI inflows.[3] But according to an informal TECC survey, Taiwan's registered investment volume – both direct and indirect – may total around (US)$1.2 billion. This estimation does not include the recently announced (US)$5 billion investment project by Taiwan's manufacturing giant Foxconn.[4] Indian data have tended to underestimate Taiwanese investment activities in the country.

A Different Investment Rationale – From Go West to Go South

Being a small island country with a population of 23 million, Taiwan has been an outward-looking economy, highly dependent on global demand for its economic growth. Taiwan enjoyed significant economic growth momentum from the 1970s to 1990s, with real GDP annual growth rate averaging about 8 per cent. Since the late 1980s, Taiwan was forced to undertake an industrial restructuring by off-shoring its labour-intensive manufacturing industries to South-East Asia and China, while promoting more value-added and technology-intensive industries at home.

With the continuous expansion of Taiwanese investment in South-East Asia and China, rapid development of the electronics and machinery industries by off-shoring their manufacturing activities across the region has not only fuelled Taiwan's economic growth in the 1990s and early 2000s but has also led to the establishment of regional production networks and value chains by Taiwan-based companies. According to the 2015 UNCTAD World Investment Report, in 2000 Taiwan's outward FDI stock was (US)$66.66 billion. In 2014 it reached (US)$258.83 billion, even larger than Korea's outward FDI stock of (US)$258.55 billion.[5]

The production networks established by Taiwan-invested manufacturing operations in China and South-East Asia have created millions of jobs across the countries. They also have helped develop manufacturing industries and made possible economic restructuring in some host countries. For example, in the 1990s, more than 2,000 Taiwanese electronics firms invested in Penang, Malaysia, helped establish one of the most important electronics clusters in South-East Asia at that time. In China, Taiwanese firms have been important players and contributed significantly to the development of various manufacturing industries, ranging from textiles and garments, footwear, toys to electronics and electrical machinery. China's eastern coastal provinces have especially benefited in their economic modernisation from the capital, technology and management knowhow brought by Taiwanese investors. These investors were important contributors to China's industrial revolution in the 1990s.

Some Taiwanese companies turned to Vietnam when the Socialist country opened its door to foreign investors in 1986 and adopted the Doi Moi or Economic Revolution Policy. In the next two decades, Taiwan remained the top foreign investor in the country. As of September 2015,

Taiwan's accumulated FDI in Vietnam reached (US)$29.34 billion, the fourth largest FDI source. Following aggressive investment action in Vietnam, Taiwanese companies also seek every opportunity of investing in other less developed ASEAN countries, mainly Cambodia and Myanmar. In May 2015, Myanmar's Ministry of Commerce opened its Representative Office in Taipei to promote bilateral trade and facilitate Taiwanese investment in the country. Different from Chinese companies which focus on mining, infrastructure and power plants, or Korean and Hong Kong investors who are more interested in real estate and natural resources, Taiwanese investors on Myanmar concentrate on manufacturing industries and related services. For example, Pou Chen Group, the world's largest branded athletic and casual footwear contract manufacturer, has established a plant in Myanmar and started operation in early 2016.

With more than two decades of investment in China and South-East Asia, Taiwanese companies have established sector-specific production networks and supply chains in the region. As a hub of ICT production, Taiwan produces more than 80 per cent of the world's notebook computers and peripherals. Some parts are made by factories in Guangdong province, China, and others in different ASEAN countries. The R&D function is maintained in the headquarters or mother companies in Taiwan. With operations in different countries, Taiwan is *de facto* participating heavily in the regional economy.

A Recent Trend – Building New Manufacturing Hubs in India

India has not been a favourable investment destination for manufacturing industries. According to DIPP, in terms of sector-wise FDI equity inflows during the period April 2000 to June 2015, services sectors (including financial, banking, insurance, business, outsourcing, R&D, courier, tech. testing and analysis, etc.) and construction development (including townships, housing, built-up infrastructure and construction-development projects) together received around 26 per cent of the FDI inflows into India, reaching around (US)$67.45 billion. FDI inflows into the manufacturing sectors were comparatively slow.

However, since the adoption of the New Manufacturing Policy in 2011 together with the Modi government's recent Make in India initiative, the years 2014/15 (April 2014 to March 2015) and first quarter of 2015/16 (April 2015 to June 2015) have seen significant growth in FDI inflows into mobile, computer software and hardware, telecommunications (including radio paging, cellular basic telephone services) and automobile industry sectors, reaching $4.76 billion, $3.29 billion and $3.66 billion respectively.[6] It appears that the government's policy is beginning to attain results.

Because of India's not so attractive investment environment for manufacturing industries, FDI inflows from Taiwan into India had been very low until the early 2000s, when India was included in an expansion programme of Taiwan government's Go South policy. The policy was first adopted in 1994 to encourage Taiwanese investment in South-East Asia by providing region-specific investment incentives and 'administrative guidance' to lead investment flows into the region, particularly in Thailand, Indonesia and the Philippines. When the policy was further expanded to India, however, most Taiwanese companies viewed India as a complementary extension to the South-East Asian region and not a potential market by itself.

It is important to note that there is a close correlation between Taiwan's interests in India and in China. Starting from the mid-2000s, when the investment environment in China began to appear less favourable as a result of wage rises and increase of other indirect production costs, some Taiwanese companies began to look outside China in search of both overseas investment destinations and new markets. Wage increase and shortage of labour in the south-east coastal provinces of China and implementation of new labour and environmental laws all drove an increasing number of Taiwanese companies away. India and some South-East Asian countries, such as Vietnam and Indonesia, hence became new attractions with their abundant workforce and relatively low wages.

According to DIPP statistics, Taiwan's total investment in India has been only around $106.4 million, representing 0.04 per cent of total investment flows received by the country during the period April 2000 to September 2015.[7] FDI outflows from Taiwan in the past few years after the global financial crisis in 2009 have, however, increased significantly. FDI amount in these years comprised more than 80 per cent of the total accumulated FDI since April 2000. This sharp growth contrasted with the consecutive decline of FDI flows from Taiwan into China since 2010, which indicated an emerging trend that Taiwanese companies are returning to South-East Asia and under this trend some are moving to India.

The trend comes at a time when Taiwanese companies have been facing increasing challenges in China. One major challenge is the rise of the Red Supply Chains, a policy adopted by the government to gradually establish Chinese supply chains by rerouting manufacturing contracts from foreign contract manufacturers to Chinese companies. To respond to this trend, in early August 2015, Foxconn Technology, also known as Hon Hai Precision Industry Group, which is the world's largest electronics contract manufacturer,[8] announced a (US)$5 billion investment project over the next five years to set up manufacturing and R&D facilities in the western Indian state of Maharashtra.[9] Foxconn closed its operations after the closure of the Nokia plant in Tamil Nadu for tax problems in 2015, but then decided to return to India with the aim of establishing its next growth engine outside China. In addition to the investment which is so far the single-largest project responding to Modi government's Make in India and Digital India initiatives, the company also announced a partnership with Japan's Soft Bank and China's Alibaba to invest in India's e-commerce player Snapdeal with a combined investment of $500 million. According to a report in *Business Standard* citing Morgan Stanley's research, India is becoming the fastest-growing e-commerce market in the world. The market is estimated to grow from $2.9 billion in 2013 to $100 billion by 2020 at a CAGR (compound annual growth rate) of about 66 per cent.

Foxconn's decision is based on India's huge market potential for smartphones and other electronic devices. India is expected to be the fastest growing smartphone market and may overtake the US smartphone market by 2017. Following the initial investment project, Foxconn may bring a cluster of its satellite suppliers and other manufacturers to India and thus create a golden opportunity for India to establish a stronger manufacturing sector centring on assembly of smartphones and other electronic devices.

Compared with China and South-East Asia, the investment activities of Taiwan's ICT industry in India are fairly recent. Most of Taiwan's leading ICT companies, including Wintek Technology, D-Link, Synnex Tec,

AsusTek Computer Inc, Acer and Benq, have established very limited presence mainly for services, sales or distribution functions due to low confidence in India as a manufacturing base. They have concerns with respect to India's poor infrastructure, lack of adequate industrial foundations and very complicated central and state-level tax and legal systems. Furthermore, due to difficulties in domestic sourcing, manufacturers have to import from other countries raw materials and semi-finished products, key components and parts. The Foxconn project, if smoothly realised, could be the first step to establish 'the mega-manufacturing hubs' in India as envisaged by Modi government's grand policy. To achieve this goal, India and Taiwan should work together to create more comprehensive industrial collaboration to take advantage of both countries' strengths in ICT industry. Taiwan's experience, technology and know-how in developing production networks and global value chains are of strategic importance to India.

Moving Towards the Next Step: The India-Taiwan Economic Cooperation Agreement (ECA) and Cooperation in the Free Trade Area of the RCEP

In January 2011, the Indian Council for Research on International Economic Relations (ICRIER) and Chung Hua Institution for Economic Research (CIER) in Taiwan signed an MoU to conduct a two-year joint study on enhancing trade, investment and economic cooperation between the two countries. In September 2013, the study report was published and presented to policymakers in India. A major finding of the study is that India and Taiwan have high complementarities in trade and industrial structure. It has therefore strongly proposed reviewing the current economic relations and taking stock of all existing barriers and obstacles, and establishing a TECC-ITA working group to examine the development of a bilateral Economic Cooperation Agreement (ECA).

According to the study, both India and Taiwan suffer from tariff and non-tariff measures. Reduction of tariff will not only bring considerable economic benefits to India, but will also help develop a stronger manufacturing sector in India by encouraging the Taiwanese business sector to invest in India. As suggested by the study, it is of timely importance to examine bilateral economic relations in the following context and consider aggressive action plans to enhance existing economic cooperation.

First, in June 2010, Taiwan and China signed an Economic Cooperation Framework Agreement (ECFA) and followed it with the conclusion of a bilateral investment agreement and service agreement and negotiations of a goods agreement. In 2013, Taiwan signed an ECA with New Zealand and Singapore respectively. India's huge potential for economic cooperation makes it a priority for Taiwan's ECA policy.

Secondly, in May 2013 ASEAN launched negotiations with its six FTA partners (China, Japan, South Korea, Australia, New Zealand and India) to develop a Regional Comprehensive Economic Partnership (RCEP). The ASEAN Economic Community (AEC) was realised at the end of 2015 to integrate ASEAN member states into a single market and single production base. The RCEP negotiation will establish the world's most populous FTA in the world, comprising 3.3 billion population. The ample supply of young labour force and an emerging middle class in the RCEP member countries promise huge benefits of the integrated regional economy. There are existing complicated regional production networks and supply chains in the region, particularly in China and some ASEAN member states such as Thailand, Malaysia and Vietnam. These regional production networks have enabled these ASEAN countries to benefit from developing manufacturing sectors and participation in the global value chains.

India adopted the Look East policy in 1991 to strengthen economic exchanges with East Asia. Though India is gradually taking part in the regional production networks, its role has not been prominent and it has mostly focused on the low level of value-addition in the region.[10] This is reflected in the low and stagnant share of manufacturing to GDP in India. India needs to enhance its role when China, ASEAN and other countries are moving towards the formation of RCEP.

India and Taiwan can work together in the regional production networks. The past three decades of industrial development and overseas investment in the region have enabled Taiwan to stand at a privileged position in the regional production networks and supply chains. Since an increasing number of Taiwanese companies are relocating their manufacturing bases away from China and consider India as a potential new Asia Factory, India and Taiwan should work together to improve productivity and quality in India's manufacturing sector. There are ample opportunities for the two sides to develop a comprehensive partnership that covers cooperation in high-value-added manufacturing industries and knowledge-based services, R&D collaboration and joint human resource development, among others. A bilateral ECA to bring down mutual trade and investment barriers can serve the purpose of India's priority policy and enable Taiwan's strengthened role in the region. Both sides should also prepare for further collaboration under RCEP in the future when the mega FTA opens for accession by new members in the region.

NOTES

1. The TECC and ITA are representative offices set up by Indian and Taiwan governments in each other's capitals, providing functions including visa application, trade and investment promotion.
2. Board of Foreign Trade, Ministry of Economic Affairs, Taiwan, http://cus93.trade.gov.tw/FSCI/
3. DIPP, http://dipp.nic.in/English/Publications/FDI_Statistics/2015/india_FDI_June2015.pdf
4. *Economic Times*, 13 January 2016, http://economictimes.indiatimes.com/tech/hardware/foxconn-to-set-up-new-facilities-in-india-in-6-months/articleshow/50567315.cms
5. UNCTADSTAT, http://unctadstat.unctad.org/wds/TableViewer/tableView.aspx
6. Fact Sheet on Foreign Direct Investment (FDI), DIPP, Ministry of Commerce and Industry, India.
7. Statement on Country-wise FDI Equity Inflows from April 2000 to September 2015, DIPP, India, http://dipp.nic.in/English/Publications/FDI_Statistics/2015/FDI_FactSheet_JulyAugustSeptember2015.pdf
8. Foxconn is the manufacturer of smartphones and tablets for mobile device players like Apple (AAPL), Samsung (SSNLF), and Xiaomi.
9. According to CAN, the Chief Minister of Maharashtra, Devendra Fadnavis, has confirmed the announcement and signed an agreement with Foxconn. It is reported that the facilities will be located either near Mumbai or Pune. 1,500 acres will be allocated for this purpose. The project is estimated to create direct jobs for 50,000 people when completed.
10. Rajat Kathuria, Global Value Chains in the Indian Context, 19 March 2013.

8

India and Taiwan: Emergence of an Economic Convergence

Suresh T. Gopalan

India and Taiwan have traversed distinctive routes as Asian nations. The two have coexisted since the middle of the 20th century. But their pathways did not intersect for along historical period that witnessed the rise and demise of the Cold War and the advent of contemporary globalisations. There have been no common geopolitical anxieties that directly concerned the two countries nor produced any form of schism between them. In fact it was a curious case of bilateral exchanges that remained dormant for half a century without any serious political or diplomatic reason or a historical legacy. This mutual exclusion was not even a product of any ideological inclinations that could have propelled these countries into different directions or leanings. Although late, the mutual rediscovery of India and Taiwan is an interesting development.

National Economic Models

The economic histories of nations are not entirely conditioned by historical factors internal to them. Conventional economic analysis focused on the domestic economic make-up to explain the variations in developmental outcomes. The emphasis was on how national economic actors, institutions and policies configured industrial relations. The resources and capabilities of native industrial classes and capitalism in general are significant in terms of ushering economic changes in society. In the immediate post-colonial years in India, this question haunted the political leadership of the country: whether the industrial classes had the capability, both industrial as well as economic, to lead the country from its industrial backwardness to modern industrial development. Nehru always held close this idea of India as a modern industrial nation emerging out of its deep-rooted religiosity. His famous euphemism for industrial plants as modern temples of India speaks volumes for his faith in the role of modern industries. When India decided to nationalise the dominant sectors of the economy such as railways, post and telecommunications, petroleum, etc., it reflected both the ideational commitment to the redistributional role of the state as well as a sober admission about the relative weakness of the native industries. The limits of the native industries were also exacerbated by conditions of economic isolations imposed by the post-war historical contingencies.

The national roots of Taiwan's passage from a largely agrarian society to an industrial leader in technological manufacturing can be traced back to a parallel set of historical factors. What was different in Taiwan from India is that the distinction between the private sector and the state was not as pronounced as in India. The greater levels of coalescence between the island's economic and political actors are easy to understand. For long decades since the establishment of the new nation, the ominous shadow of dismemberment loomed large over the island. Historical compulsions have forced Taiwan to adapt to a political model that stressed convergence between state and society and between economy and political institutions. Taiwan inherited historical conditions that enabled it to rise in the future as a far more coherent political and economic system. As in the case of India, the post-war historical contingencies have created conditions of isolation for Taiwan too. But the country was able to overcome this force of circumstances as it had developed forward economic linkages with advanced industrial regions, most notably with the United States. As Formosa (as Taiwan was then known) was drawn into the lager geopolitical contestation between the US and the Communist mainland China, it was at the same time drawn into a trans-continental economic circuit fashioned by advanced industrial nations. Taiwan was able to develop global economic linkages much earlier than India.

Two Economic Regions

Another dimension that explains the variance between India and Taiwan is the regional economic characteristics. The South Asian region to which India belongs shared largely similar economic characteristics. India and its neighbours are predominantly agrarian societies with restricted development of modern industries. In fact, India represents the leading economic region in comparison to others. Except India, most South Asian countries have limited linkages with global economic flows. The participation of the South Asian nations in international trade is marginal. Above all, politics driven by primordial affinities often inhibit these countries from the path of economic development. Continued geopolitical rivalries prevent them from possibilities of economic integration or creating open trade linkages. Despite modest developmental indices, open market integration can create greater economic benefits. The restricted trade, protected domestic market and extremely limited inter-regional connectivity are holding back South Asia from developing the regional economy. Until now the political elite and the economic actors in South Asia have not shown any serious impulse towards developing trans-regional linkages in terms of markets, production networks or infrastructures. Therefore South Asia has entered the 21st century with all the historical baggage it inherited from the past institutional structures, cultural make-up and agrarian backwardness. The regional identity of South Asia is moulded primarily by ethno-geographical factors which continue to produce internal dissensions.

Taiwan presents a distinctive case of how a nation can overcome its historically imposed geopolitical constraints through adapting to rational economic choices. Certain parallels between Taiwan and India are striking. Taiwan is located both geographically as well as culturally in a regional civilisation derived deeply from Chinese values. While values can be historically relative and are subject to adaptations from outside, their derivative roots prove to be far more resilient in fostering those values for the future. Taiwan cannot really claim any distinctive national or cultural identity as it belongs to the geo-civilisational sphere of Confucian China. The people of Taiwan and the people of Fujian and Guangdong provinces of mainland China share close ethnic affinities, common language, religion and customs. These ties were temporarily broken and remained dormant for four decades since the establishment of the People's Republic in the mainland and the Republic of Taiwan in the island in 1949. However, as cultural factors are far more resilient forces, the shared ethnic and linguistic affinities between the people in the mainland and Taiwan revived and were restored into historical continuities. Since the reforms and opening up in the mainland, we see vigorous integrative tendencies sweeping aside the historical geopolitical schism that existed for long, thus paving the way for economic integration too.

How Taiwan achieved economic integration with the mainland despite differences over governing norms ought to be a significant point for the political elites in South Asia. Is religious dissension more difficult to surmount than ideational ruptures, as demonstrated through the two cases? The religious dissension between India and Pakistan shows no signs of ebbing. It continues to reverberate in all ranges of exchanges between the two countries, including economic and cultural. At times it provokes serious conventional tensions too. But the ideational incongruities between Taiwan and the mainland now appear to be fleeting in their histories that elapsed when the cultural affinities were revived. Besides, economic integration between Taiwan and the mainland is made possible by two different governing models. The differences over political and institutional norms are not critical conditioning factors against economic exchanges.

India and Taiwan: Converging Asian Economies

The economic rediscovery between India and Taiwan was made possible largely by the structural changes brought about by global economic processes. During the long planning era, India remained essentially a national economy with limited economic interactions with the rest of the world. As indicated earlier, it was not that the highly regulation-driven state constrained the domestic economic sectors from developing forward linkages with the foreign investors. Rather, the national industries lacked adequate technological capabilities and organisational flexibility to adapt to respond to the competition from foreign companies. Some of these anxieties can be gauged from the policy advocacy of the Federation of Indian Chambers of Commerce and Industry (FICCI) during the 1990s. It is also pertinent to note that regulation was a key concern for both the government and the domestic industry. For the government, regulation was a basic normative field as well as an enduring institutional practice that strived to make India a more self-reliant economy. For the private industry, it meant excessive control over entrepreneurialism that was responsible for economic stagnation. But during the immediate post-reform years when India was becoming more inclined to open the market for foreign investment, the private business demanded protection from the government as the large global corporations controlled far greater leverage in technology, capital and production capabilities against which the Indian companies were not able to compete on an equal footing. India's reform decade was a period of anxieties shared by the private business, the state and social groups who sensed the reforms as potent agents of vulnerabilities. These concerns provoked deeply emotive responses from a cross-section of society, forcing the government to follow an incremental approach to the reforms.

In contrast, economic globalisation did not provoke any social dissension in China. Since Taiwan's political models from its inception were seen as the other of the mainland in ideational as well as institutional orientations, market liberalism never caused any anxieties among the social classes. Moreover, with long exposure to the market liberalism of the Western world, Taiwan had developed significant linkages with the global economy, especially in technological upgradations. Another factor was the corporatist governance model, where interest articulations by different social and professional groups were largely state mediated. The question of regulation did not arise in policy debates as it did in the case of India. In other words, Taiwan did not inherit any economic institutions or norms that were resistant to globalisation or foreign origin.

Taiwan's economic pathways are shaped by three important factors. First is the locational advantage. The island nation belongs to the East Asian economic region comprised of mainland China, Japan and South Korea. Although these nations have been governed by vastly different political ideas and institutional models for a long time, there have been strong integrative economic tendencies that brought them into direct interactions more than ever before. The region was sharply divided by geopolitical anxieties inherited from the historical legacies of World War II, Japanese militarism, Communist revolution, and the Cold War. These historical events have left deep scars among the people of mainland China, Taiwan and South Korea. But in the closing decades of the 20th century, Taiwan and mainland China were able to overcome the burden of historical memories. The economic interactions that followed in subsequent years helped them to rediscover their common cultural roots and they were able to imagine a shared destiny in the economic arena. Although there are lingering geopolitical apprehensions often precipitated by Japan and mainland China, East Asia remains one of the most peaceful, stable and economically advancing regions of the world.

Since the mid-1980s, economic researchers and business analysts have pointed to the emergence of a common economic region comprising mainland China, Hong Kong and Taiwan. What prompted them to imagine the rise of an integrated economic region were the historical convergences of a complex set of factors providing comparative advantages to each of these three regions. China had enormous raw material resources and low-wage labour. With the dissolution of the rural communes in the late 1970s and the exhaustion of the Household Responsibility System during the early 1980s, China was left with no significant economic sector that could absorb the population into any form of employment, thus creating a vast pool of surplus labour. The large-scale rural-to-urban migration that began around this time made available a social stratum which can be called a precarious multitude, which thronged to cities in search of wage-earning opportunities. The creation of low-wage labour enabled China to then embark on the path of labour-intensive industrialisation. Hong Kong by then had developed extensive trade links with the leading economic regions of the world. The city was also known for specialised international financial services. Besides, Hong Kong emerged as a key transport hub well connected in the maritime trade circuits. Taiwan had gained substantial experience in labour-intensive manufacturing in textiles, apparels and electronics, which gave it a special edge over others in manufacturing technology and new managerial expertise. During the

1980s, owing to the labour shortage and negative exchange rate between the US dollar and the Taiwan dollar, the island nation had started restructuring the domestic industrial base, moving away from labour-intensive sectors to more technology-oriented manufacturing and began to search for investment opportunities elsewhere. In fact, when the mainland introduced economic reforms, Taiwan was all set for foreign investment, which also made possible the relocation of its labour-intensive sectors to China, in particular Guangdong and Fujian provinces, where the Taiwanese have close ethnic ties as well as native-place affinities.

The dense economic interpenetration between Guangdong and Fujian provinces in the mainland, Taiwan and Hong Kong have created a regional economic system that brought these regions ever closer to each other in economic and socio-cultural exchanges, if not in the political sphere. Scholars have used different descriptive and analytical categories to refer to the growing economic and spatial integrations among these three regions, such as Greater China Common Market, Greater Chinese Economic Community, etc. Xiangming Chen used the term Greater South China Economic Region 'to characterise the special economic relations and the new spatial division of labour among China's Guangdong and Fujian provinces, Hong Kong and Taiwan'.

Secondly, as indicated earlier, Taiwan benefited enormously from the opening of the Chinese economy in terms of a new outlet for Taiwanese capital investment, relocation of manufacturing sectors, access to China's low wage labour, raw material resources and, above all, to the vast mainland market. Thirdly, the economies of these countries are interpenetrated by each other's, thus creating a densely integrated transnational economic sphere. Taiwan has significant levels of investments in Guangdong and Fujian provinces and more specifically in the factory towns of Dongguan, Shenzhen and Guangzhou.

As an economic region, the characteristic features of South Asia are in sharp contrast to that of the Greater China Economic Region or, for that matter, East Asia. We have examined earlier how regional dissensions cyclically breed from historical and geopolitical contestations that inhibit the developmental processes. Without returning to these questions again, we can identify one of the salient markers of combined underdevelopment in South Asia, which is the stranglehold of religious identities over popular consciousness or, in other words, the extraordinary resilience of primordialism in politics. I would posit that the reasons for development variance between India and Taiwan can partly be explained in terms of the limited transformative impulses towards economic aspiration and the overriding influence of culturally given identities of religion, language and caste.

In India, since the advent of economic reforms, this longing for development has been finding ever more expression in popular as well as policy frameworks. Although there are intermittent outbreaks of identity-based political mobilisations, it appears that finally a more modernist imagination of economic transformation has come to define the popular mind. Alongside a language of politics that appeals more to the developmental needs, it is finding poplar resonance and has to some extent led to the waning of religious mobilisations. These shifting contours of the Indian polity as well as public policy orientations were most visibly manifest in the two terms of the United Progressive Alliance (UPA) governments steered by the economist Manmohan Singh as Prime Minister. During its two terms in office the UPA was able to bring economic questions to the fore of the Indian political processes. The idea of development became a key word in national debates that brought about a new orientation to the processes of public policymaking. In fact, India made the crucial transition from a central planning and regulated regime to that of a largely deregulated market economy. More significantly, there was a profound ideational shift towards market capitalism, long resisted by the political and social classes in India.

The National Democratic Alliance (NDA) government of Prime Minister Narendra Modi, which assumed office in 2014, has unveiled an ambitious economic plan. I would outline two components of the new economic policy to underscore the policy continuities broadening the scope of the economic reforms carried out by the previous UPA governments. In terms of the broader objectives, the new policies are formulated to promote what has been called the 'ease of doing business' in India. This comprises a set of new policy directives aimed to reduce the administrative and procedural bottlenecks with regard to starting and running business in India. The existing industrial policy rooted in the planning era is perceived to be inhibitive to private entrepreneurialism and therefore an anachronism in an increasingly globalising world. It is therefore imperative to increase the speed in the completion of procedures pertaining to setting up companies in India. The government has announced specific measures to simplify the procedures relating to setting up industries and also compliance requirements.

The second component is the Make in India initiative. Launched in September 2015, it focuses on the revival of India's manufacturing sector, thereby to make India a manufacturing powerhouse. It actively encourages and seeks foreign companies to increase their investment in India's manufacturing sector. Make in India became a policy campaign with the twin objectives to attract overseas companies to set up production facilities in India, and also encourage domestic companies to increase production within the country. The initiative will be promoted through the newly created National Investment and Manufacturing Zones. There are interesting models outlined for the promotion of Make in India such as Industrial Townships, which will function like self-governing and autonomous units without being subjected to government intervention or regulations.

The new industrial policies also seek to transform the system of labour regulation that post-reform India inherited from the planning era. Indian business associations and liberal critics have been demanding labour reforms as a prerequisite for industrial growth as they hold the existing regulatory regime responsible for the labour market rigidities. The UPA government's labour policy was one of cautious ambivalence towards legislation while introducing incremental reforms in select areas. The NDA government's approach to the labour question marks a decisive shift from that of the earlier governments. The objectives of the new policy seem to be full-scale legal reforms which, if approved by Parliament, will bring an end to the era of labour regulations in the formal sector.

After a quarter century since the introduction of economic reforms, India seems to have finally entered into a market economy largely freed from regulations in many areas and that converges with global capital flows. A new historical setting has been created for the Indian economy. It might appear anachronistic for India to pursue labour-intensive industrialisation at a time when the East Asian countries are already well past that stage. But for Taiwan this moment offers new possibilities. For three decades Taiwan's foreign investments concentrated in the Greater China region where there are already visible signs of an industrial stagnation. A new economic convergence between India and Taiwan can develop fortuitously out of the present Asian economic relations.

9

India-Taiwan Economic Relations and the China Factor: Prospects of Synergies and Challenges for Regional Economic Integration

Aravind Yelery

'Everything but Taiwan' (EBT) rhetoric is proving futile and unjustifiable for mainland communist leaders in the wake of ongoing debates on regional economic integrations, especially when the Chinese economy is struggling to keep up its momentum. With political controversies surrounding the legal status of one-China, Taiwan was forced to be excluded from Asia-Pacific Economic Cooperation (APEC).[1] Moreover, EBT remained a dominant factor as far as Taiwan's participation in the process of ASEAN's economic integration was concerned. For Taiwan, the political isolation was not as severe as the economic loss. Though Taiwan has smartly compensated its economic loss through a variety of bilateral economic modalities, which include investments and special trade arrangements, Taiwan's future is tied up with the progress of regional mechanisms in East Asia and Asia-Pacific. Recently, the US-led partnership covering pan-Pacific trade partners eschewed Taiwan's prospects and once the agreement enters into practice, Taiwan's trade share with these countries will be adversely affected. However, with the ongoing transformation in the global dynamics of economic integration and slowdown of China's economy, China's best chances to monetise are at stake. With its close linkages with the regional partners, Taiwan maintains the ability to work as a deal breaker in the intra-regional trade setups. While China attempts economic integration in East Asia and Asia-Pacific, Taiwan turns out to be China's and perhaps Asia's best bet.

While the Taiwanese Dug Deep in the Chinese Market, China Influenced Global Business

The political, ideological and historical origins of mistrust resulted in stifling the development of cross-Strait relations. These cross-Strait tensions did impact Taiwan's global economic and trade exchanges. This also was used by the Chinese to limit Taiwan's economic expansion in the region by designing its exclusion from various negotiations on regional collaboration, forcing Taiwan's economic integration with mainland China and undermining its autonomy.

Taiwan, with a prominent presence in technology-dominated industries, seems to be losing its regional linkages. On the one hand, Chinese industries populated the global markets with giveaway prices as the world's Original Equipment Manufacturer (OEM) and on the other hand, its cross-Strait counterparts from Taiwan remained confident about their technical standards and concentrated more on tech-intensive markets.[2] Taiwan had its stint as the home for OEMs but changed its course to technology-driven industries when global business was revolutionised due to the rise of information communication technologies (ICT). With this, Taiwan maintained a unique portfolio both in labour- and capital-intensive industries as well as scaled equally well in non-tech and tech type of products. Going a step ahead, Taiwanese entrepreneurs established their factories in mainland China to save on the production cost.[3] Taiwanese investment in mainland China maintained an upward momentum because of the mainland's abundant labour force, vast market, low land rents, geographical proximity, availability of raw materials, and similarities in culture and language.

As a result of these trends, over the past 25 years, Taiwan's reliance on China's economy has gone from negligible to substantial. At present, 70 percent of Taiwan's GDP comprises of exports, 40 percent of which go to China, making Taiwan over-reliant on a single export market.[4] Taiwan's vulnerability is quite broad: it relies upon China as the number one market for its exports, the number one venue for its foreign investment and the number one production base for many of its most profitable exports, especially its ICT exports. Top Taiwanese brands such as Asustek Computer, Trend Micro, HTC, and Acer expanded their brand presence in China. Taiwanese entrepreneurs relied heavily on the business interdependency in and beyond the region. The obvious effects of the slowing of the Chinese economy can be noticed on the Taiwanese economy.

This development can be viewed from two different perspectives – one, brands from the island flourished deep inside mainland China and grew stronger and second, China facilitated this inter-dependency to grow. While most conspiracy theorists through their traditional approach viewed this economic engagement as a trap, Murray Scot Tanner, a leading theorist, believed that if China were able to close down key parts of this economic relationship, Taiwan would be vulnerable to a major recession and other severe forms of economic dislocation.[5] However, this did not happen the way most observers believed. In the last few years, endogenous factors have threatened the prospects of both countries. The slowing down of their economies means that much is at stake for China and Taiwan and, moreover, lack of any regional economic integration invites a set of other variants of external threats.

Is Taiwan China's Best Bet in Regional Integration?

Taiwan's economy is going through some rough patches, with recession in exports and foreign investment[6] contrasted by high inflation.[7] The impact will grow much severe if Taiwan does not change its macroeconomic alignments. This includes protecting from trade and business vulnerabilities. The best solution the Taiwanese could think of is to be part of the multilateral economic setup. Apart from deepening cross-Strait economic cooperation, the Taiwanese are under pressure to pay more attention to the integration of the industrial value chain which the multilateral trade would offer them. So far, China has blocked Taiwan's entry into a number of regional and multilateral forums in an attempt at restricting Taiwan's influence. However, as mentioned, the growing complexities within global integrations of production and value chains would make China not to go on ostrich-like. A Taiwan Institute of Economics quantitative analysis shows that if Taiwan joins the Regional Comprehensive Economic Partnership (RCEP), GDP growth rate will increase by 4.36 percent.[8] As per statistics, if Taiwan remains out of any larger trade agreements, the impact will be severe.

Taiwan's Significance in Asia-Pacific

Taiwan has pursued its trade policy with growing transparency. Along with its market share and trade volumes, the value of intangible assets like trademarks and copyrighted goods allowed Taiwan to maintain its place in the global supply chain (GSC). For example, the RCEP market accounts for 57 percent of Taiwan's foreign trade. As a result, Taiwan is a part of multiple regional trade networks and its importance to any new trade agreements (i.e. RCEP) or partnerships (i.e. TPP) would not come at the expense of any of the existing members. More than the aspirations of Taiwan to align with pan-Asia or pan-Asia-Pacific regional trade frameworks, it is Taiwan's partners who aspire for it to play a critical role in regional economic integration.[9] On the one hand, the East Asia Free Trade Area, RCEP, etc. will be crucial for the survival of Taiwan's foreign trade. Taiwan is also an advanced economy in the Asia-Pacific region, a significant trader which makes it a prominent state in evolving ideas of economic multilateralism and integration of business interests.

How China May Benefit from Taiwan's Position in the Region

China's growing intentions to give Taiwan a prominent place in the East Asian as well as pan-Asia-Pacific regional trade partnerships are evident from the present trajectory of business and domestic economic challenges. Under pressure, China may accept Taiwan as the additional or +1 member if the latter accepts China's leadership in RCEP. China is aware that Taiwan's compliance record is better than that of the mainland and that is the main reason behind Taiwan's prominence in ICT-related exports. The 'Everyone but Taiwan' rhetoric does not stand effective in the ever-growing complex scenario of newer preferential policies being pursued by China and the US in their respective peripheral areas. Taiwan's isolation also means impending effects on trade and investments. On a more serious note, for the Chinese, leaving Taiwan's economic development in a state of predicament means allowing the next generation of new rules and trade systems, which will eventually dominate the world's major trade and investment relations, to arrive early. It will change the direction of capital flow by affecting investment and production. As a double effect, the weaknesses and strengths of Taiwan's economy and trade are directly correlated with China's prospects in pursuing successful regional economic integration. Taiwan is important to global manufacturing supply chains and strategically important to key export supply chains in Asia-Pacific. China needs to take a more respectful and reciprocal stand towards trade partners, including India and Taiwan.

Repositioning of India-Taiwan Economic Ties

Even though India officially acknowledges one-China policy and does not recognise Taiwan as a state, over the years it has developed strong economic ties with Taiwanese counterparts. Taiwan's trade with India looks minimal compared to China's,[10] but it has competitiveness in a number of areas which might affect China's position in India. The Chinese trade structure may face fierce competition if the Taiwanese start disinvesting from China and look for alternative geography in Asia. While Chinese companies continue to look for more space in the Indian market, the trade dominated in the areas of commodities, reactors, boilers, machinery, electric machinery, sound equipment, etc.; organic chemicals; ores and cotton,[11] whereas the Taiwanese companies are progressively looking to invest in India in areas such as nano-technology, semiconductors, aviation and space, satellite development, biotechnology, and agriculture.[12] The trade and economic ties with Taiwan are unique and offer India unbounded opportunities to cooperate with Taiwan.

Tsai Ing-wen (蔡英文), who won the recently held Taiwanese presidential elections and has been Taiwan's Deputy Prime Minister, in one of her interviews gave a sketch of Taiwan's shifting economic priorities. She pointed out how Taiwan should sway away from China independently and look for areas which have more potential, including ASEAN and India.[13] Tsai further termed the major trade blocs' and ASEAN's decision to keep Taiwan away from a free trade agreement (FTA) as 'unfortunate'. Taiwanese investors and exporters have no FTA benefits or protections in ASEAN. Tsai cleverly puts down that the Taiwanese companies are growing wiser and have expanded from exporting goods to exporting capital. She also mentioned that

> '[N]ow we are beginning to export services, talent and capital. We want to make our economy more competitive by establishing closer links with ASEAN countries. We want to encourage our investors to go south. They have been very successful going west to China but as the labour cost rose we think that ASEAN is full of opportunity. We are probably second or third largest investor in ASEAN countries but it seems that sometimes this is forgotten and that we are only remembered for our investments in China.'[14]

While explaining how the 'non-inclusive' can be overcome, she answered, 'it may turn out that we are excluded from the free trade agreement but I am confident our companies are flexible enough to explore further trade and investment opportunities in the region. India and the Middle East are also regions we want to increase trade with and feel our economy is complementary to these places.'[15] It is not a surprise that Taiwan's engagement started with such pragmatic approach. It was during Ms. Tsai's Deputy Prime Ministership that Taiwan and India signed a memorandum of understanding (MoU) in April 2007 agreeing to cooperate in the fields of science and technology.[16] Earlier, an agreement on the Promotion and Protection of Investment was concluded between the two sides, which came into force in 2005, that laid the foundation of bilateral investment.[17] Taiwan's growing interest in India was further triggered when its FTA prospects with ASEAN looked gloomy and China started pursuing the ambitious RCEP agenda.

India's Look East policy terms Taiwan as one of the catalysts to ensure a growing cross-competency building.[18] As the policy grew more mature and Taiwan's need to pursue economic ties with non-mainland entities intensified, it led to a new turn in cross-sectoral engagements between India and Taiwan. Non-inclusion and further delay in getting FTA deals with ASEAN eventually left Taiwan with limited negotiating room. As a result, Taiwan started looking to pursue its FTA with non-ASEAN member countries more aggressively. India also, being a non-ASEAN member and the state which was included in the RCEP's earlier frameworks, created the environment to venture together. Tying up with the Indian industry also was seen as essential in the wake of accelerating talks related to RCEP and TPP. With the emerging macroeconomic complementarities in India (business environment, reforms in trade-related regulations), Michael Lin (林慶鑫), the director of the Taiwan External Trade Development Council's (TAITRA) branch office in Mumbai, believes that Taiwan can optimise its trade relations with India and contribute towards India's campaign to make India a leader in global manufacturing.[19] For political reasons, the ups and downs in the India-China trade let Taiwanese companies emerge as the net gainer. Taiwan's exports to India grew from (US)$642 million in 2001 to $3 billion in 2015.[20] The total trade between the two sides grew from $1.2 billion in 2000 to $4.9 billion in 2015. The bulging manufacturing sector offers more opportunities for Taiwan, making it the sole beneficiary, with Taiwan enjoying a trade surplus of $1.1 billion in 2015.[21] India is now Taiwan's 16th-largest export market.[22] While Taiwan's pool of exports was further strengthened beyond East Asia and South East Asia, its exports to China scored lower than the previous years. During the last 10 years (2005-2015), Taiwan's trade with China has gone through significant volatilities. From 2001 to 2005, Taiwan's exports to China increased by approximately three times, from $33.8 billion in 2001 to $78.3 billion in 2005. However, from 2006-2015, exports witnessed slower growth, from $90 billion in 2006 to $112.5 billion in 2015.[23] The latest data on Taiwan's exports to China in January 2016 confirm that Taiwan is losing its grip over exports to China. The exports volume (to China) in January 2016 was at its four years' low.[24]

More than the trade volume, India would look to Taiwan as a partner in fulfilling the vacuum in the areas of hardware technologies and combine it with its specialties in space sciences and services. Taiwanese companies have signed an agreement with the Indian state, Karnataka, to set up an industrial hub. The MoU with the Taiwan Electrical and Electronic Manufacturers' Association (TEEMA) to set up a Taiwan Electronic Manufacturing Cluster (TEMC) aims to bolster the hardware manufacturing in India.[25] Apart from the initiative in setting up the hub, Indian industries look at Taiwanese expertise in tooling and related industries, which would support the rise of India's manufacturing sector. More importantly, the machine tools industry has the potential to play a catalysing role in Indian manufacturing. Chinese companies are struggling to make their own space in this segment but India has been Taiwan's traditional market, with German companies as its rival. The instant growth in the Chinese auto industry also owes its success to Taiwanese hardware industry.[26] The Taiwanese are selective in their bases in India and are seen implementing their India plan with precision. For instance, in December 2012, Taiwan was allowed to establish a branch office of the Taipei Economic and Cultural Center (TECC) in Chennai, a major auto cluster in India and heading to be another major software/IT services city in the country. Another example of Taiwan's growing presence can be measured from the fact that Taiwanese banks are evaluating the prospects of operating out of India. Like the China Development Bank is spearheading Chinese investments in India, along with other nationalised banks, Taiwan's financial services industry is also expanding its presence in India in order to help finance new ventures in India. CTBC – China Trust Bank – has started operating in India irrespective of the difficulties in obtaining branch licences and a lengthy approval process.[27] The need for capital has made India more lucrative to enter and also fund its own compatriots. Moreover, these banks benefit from better interest margins since the lending rate in India averages about 10 percent.[28]

Is a China-India-Taiwan Model Underway?

Both India and Taiwan have subtle opportunities to seize while new regional economic partnerships are being shaped in Asia-Pacific. China has to keep a close watch on how and where it could complement and value-add. Taiwan, which is not a part of either TPP or RCEP, has a lot to offer in terms of global chains of production and supply, as discussed. By aligning Taiwanese business with itself, China would slow down the recession in its growth. Moreover, dismayed by TPP's response and the post-formalised threats in terms of standards and preferential policies, the Taiwanese would look for more Chinese help to secure a strong position in the RCEP and other East Asian regional economic architectures. India is a value-add to China-Taiwan relations and this will help the three countries seek more opportunities to work together.

In the current global trading environment, regional agreements such as RCEP present the most viable opportunities for countries to liberalise trade barriers. Taiwan's and India's participation in RCEP will contribute to the process wherein the efforts related to regional integration – including RCEP – may enable an FTA that covers the entire Asia-Pacific region. In an effort to expand their global production network (GPN), Taiwanese companies are growingly inclined to use India as their manufacturing base to enter into South Asia and the Middle East. There are a number of areas such as auto parts, electronics, tyres, accessories, precision tools, etc. which await investments from Taiwanese companies. Taiwan also remains one of the emerging frontiers for global businesses which have invested in India as a part of their GPN to enter the Taiwanese market. The foreign brands made in India are looking for Taiwanese market. The Volkswagen Polo is a good example. It is cheaper by 200,000 TND and is causing more price wars in the Taiwanese auto market. A few years ago, Tata's Nano had created the same tension in the world's Silicon Valley for auto spare parts and tooling systems.[29] Indian entrepreneurs and auto industry clusters in and around Pune-Pimpri-Chinchwad and Chennai are growing dependent on Taiwanese tooling systems and auto parts, but the dynamics are changing rapidly in the auto industry.

Conclusion: Dividends Unexplored

There are certain areas such as innovation and start-ups, where India may prefer Taiwan when it comes to 'Make in India'. Taiwan's president-elect, Tsai Ying-wen, who is yet to take charge, had announced during her campaign about the new 'go south' agenda, favouring ties with India and South East Asia. The earlier version of 'go south', launched during the rule of President Lee Teng-hui in 1994, emphasised trade links with ASEAN and, to a lesser extent, India. The Western, Japanese and Korean companies' increasing interest in the South East Asian countries also forced the Taiwanese enterprises to prefer other regions but India was a less significant destination.[30] Tsai's new policy is seen as an attempt to wean

Taiwan's economy away from the excessive reliance on China built up during the government of President Ma Ying-jeou.[31] Unlike the Chinese way of diversifying its industries across the Asian region and lookout for the market, the Taiwanese have trickier questions to solve. Not being recognised as a political entity, Taiwan has been silently playing its own part in the global chain of economic interdependencies. If any economic integration has to be successful in the larger Asian economic theatre, it has to happen with more synergies being explored among these three partners. Mere marginalisation of capital and goods based on the political interest would deter the natural progress of such integrations.

As Taiwan and China are looking for more space in the Indian subcontinent, the search for complementarities becomes critical for the parties involved. Since both these economies have a varied sectoral appetite in India, India is adopting a multi-pronged approach to monetise. India's interest in the Chinese and Taiwanese markets has been varied. While the Chinese are taking more interest in collaborating with public infrastructure projects, occupying more space in the services industry (mainly hospitality) and mass clustering, the Taiwanese companies are specialising in innovation-led technologies and soft skills, which gels well with the upper valley of product and system integration. The transforming manufacturing may bring more Taiwanese presence in India. While the whole debate on regional economic integrations heats up and materialises, India, China and Taiwan would lose time to catch up with the other economically integrated regions. So the question is not when but how fast these three economies pull their weight and materialise these synergies. All three economies can benefit from relocating their business interest in each other and push the collective economic viabilities. The problem lies in the one-size-fits-all economic and political preferences which hold them back from exploring more dividends of interlinking markets. There is no single recipe, but all three partners must grasp one fact: doing business is not what it used to be, marginalised and politically oriented.

NOTES

1. *China Daily*, 'APEC to handle Chinese Taipei under "one-China policy"', 20 November 2008, http://www.chinadaily.com.cn/china/2008-11/20/content_7225368.htm (accessed on 21 December 2015).

2. Chris Hung, 'Outlook of Taiwanese ICT industry: current status and development strategies', 20 August 2015, www.cieca.org.tw/ConferenceData.aspx?mrid=704 (accessed on 25 January 2016); Andrew Jeffreys (ed.), *The Report: Taiwan 2007,* Oxford Business Group, 2007, ISBN 1-90202339-78-9.
3. *China Daily*, 'Taiwan firms face rising labor costs', 22 June 2010, http://www.chinadaily.com.cn/china/2010-06/22/content_10005273.htm (accessed on 20 December 2015).
4. Ministry of Finance, Republic of China, 2016. 'External trade statistics: export and import value by country', http://www.mof.gov.tw/Eng/Pages/Detail.aspx?nodeid=259&pid=64520 (accessed on 16 March 2016); Crystal Hsu, 'Taiwan likely in recession: economists', 26 September 2015, http://www.taipeitimes.com/News/biz/archives/2015/09/26/2003628584 (accessed on 2 February 2016); Sophia Yan, 'Trade has turned China and Taiwan into frenemies', CNN Money, 5 November 2015, http://money.cnn.com/2015/11/05/news/china-taiwan-trade-economy/ (accessed on 25 February 2016).
5. Murray Scot Tanner, *Chinese Economic Coercion against Taiwan: A Tricky Weapon to Use*, Santa Monica: RAND, 2007, p. 137, http://www.rand.org/content/dam/rand/pubs/monographs/2007/RAND_MG507.pdf.
6. *World Economic Survey* report, published by *Taipei Times* on 11 February 2016, reported that 'exports may stagnate at 5.5 in the coming six months'. 'Taiwan's economy deteriorating: Ifo,' 13 February 2016, http://www.taipeitimes.com/News/biz/archives/2016/02/13/2003639279 (accessed on 23 February 2016).
7. According to the Directorate-General of Budget, Accounting and Statistics, Taiwan, consumer prices in Taiwan rose to 2.40 in February 2016. It is the highest inflation rate since February 2013. 'Taiwan inflation rate', Trading Economics, Mach 2016,http://www.tradingeconomics.com/taiwan/inflation-cpi (accessed on 15 March 2016).
8. Wu Fucheng, 'Qianzhan RCEP dui taiwan de jihuiyutiaozhan' (前瞻 RCEP 對台灣的機會與挑戰) [A review of opportunities and challenges for Taiwan by joining RCEP], *Pacific Ocean Enterprise Forum Brief*, March 2014, No. 3, http://www.ctpecc.org.tw/publications/PECC-201403.pdf (accessed on 10 February 2016).
9. Economics Online/Importers and Exporters Association of Taipei, 'Buronghushi de RCEP zhenghechongji li' (不容忽視的 RCEP 整合衝擊力) [RCEP integration's impact cannot be ignored] May 2013., no. 264, http://www.ieatpe.org.tw/magazine/ebook264/b5.pdf (accessed on 13 February 2016); Wu Fucheng, 'Jiaru RCEP de tiaozhanyuchulu' (加入 RCEP 的挑戰與出路) [Join the RCEP: challenges and solutions], 6 November 2012, http://www.cnfi.org.tw/kmportal/front/bin/ptdetail.phtml?Part=magazine10111-512-4 (accessed on 23 February 2016); Li Woqiang, 'Taiwan jiaru TPP yu RCEP de jihuiyutiaozhan' (台灣加入TPP,與 RCEP 的機會與挑戰) [Taiwan's entry into TPP and RCEP: opportunities and challenges], 26 March 2014, http://www.npf.org.tw/1/13404 (accessed on 10 February 2016); Min Qing, 'Mayingjiu: TPPyu RCEP yingshuangguibingjin' (马英九：TPP与 RCEP 应双轨并进) [Ma Ying Jiu: Taiwan should adopt dual-track approach to TPP and RCEP], 17 February 2014, http://www.epochtimes.com/gb/14/2/17/n4085537.htm, (accessed on 10 February 2016).
10. In 2015, China's trade with India was at (US)$71.22 billion (*Economics Times,* 2016),

whereas Taiwan's trade with India stood at $4.95 billion (Ministry of Finance, Republic of China, 2016).

11. Embassy of India, Beijing, 2013. 'India-China bilateral relations: trade & commercial relations', http://www.indianembassy.org.cn/DynamicContent.aspx?MenuId=3&SubMenuId=0 (accessed on 26 February 2016).
12. Jeffreys, *The Report: Taiwan 2007,* n. 2.
13. Ibid., p. 10.
14. Ibid.
15. Ibid.
16. T.N. Ashok, 'India Taiwan bilateral relations set to expand further: Taiwan envoy to India', 4 June 2015, http://diplomacyindia.com/india-taiwan-bilateral-relations-set-to-expand-further-taiwan-envoy-to-india-3639/ (accessed on 21 February 2016).
17. Ibid.
18. Ibid.
19. Kelly Her, 'New roads to India', *Taiwan Review,* 1 February 2016, http://taiwantoday.tw/ct.asp?xItem=241379&ctNode=2235&mp=9 (accessed on 2 February 2016).
20. Ministry of Finance, ROC, 'External trade statistics ...', n. 4.
21. Ibid.
22. *Taiwan Today,* 'New roads to India', 1 February 2016, www.taiwantoday.tw/fp.asp?xItem=241379&CtNode=2178 (accessed on 12 March 2016); *China Post,* 'Taiwan and India seeking to bolster trade relations', 1 May. 2015, http://www.chinapost.com.tw/taiwan-business/2015/05/01/434911/Taiwan-and.htm (accessed on 11 March 2016).
23. Ministry of Finance, ROC, 'External trade statistics ...', n. 4.
24. Ibid.
25. Pradeesh Chandran, 'Taiwanese Cos to invest Rs. 3,200 cr in electronic cluster in Karnataka', *The Hindu*, 12 April 2015, http://www.thehindu.com/news/national/karnataka/taiwanese-cos-to-invest-rs-3200-cr-in-electronic-cluster-in-karnataka/article7530747.ece (accessed on 20 December 2015).
26. Moneycontrol.com, 'Taiwanese cos keen to be part of Make in India project', 13 April 2015, http://www.moneycontrol.com/news/press-release/taiwanese-cos-keen-to-be-partmakeindia-project_2508481.html (accessed on 22 December 2015).
27. CTBC Bank opened its first branch in New Delhi in 1996 and its second branch in Sriperumbudur, Chennai in 2012. 'Welcome to CTBC Bank Co. Ltd.', http://www.chinatrustindia.com(accessed on 3 March 2016). Areport by the Reserve Bank of India in early 2016 says that CTBC Bank is the only Taiwanese bank which has a branch form of presence in India, https://www.rbi.org.in/commonman/Upload/English/Content/PDFs/71207.pdf.
28. *Taiwan Today,* 'New roads to India', 1 February 2016, www.taiwantoday.tw/fp.asp?xItem=241379&CtNode=2178 (accessed on 12 March 2016).
29. *TVBS News,* 'Yinduchegong tai! Tong kuan chechajia '20 wan' (印度車」攻台！同款車差價「20萬」) [Indian cars 'to attack' Taiwan! Car models with the difference of 200,000 TND], 10 February 2014, http://news.tvbs.com.tw/old-news.html?nid=520662 (accessed on 20 March 2016).

30. Bruce Einhorn, 'Taiwanese Go South', 6 November 1995, http://www.bloomberg.com/news/articles/1995-11-05/taiwanese-go-south-intl-edition (accessed on 10 March 2016).
31. Matthew Strong, 'Tsai unveils Go South policy,' *Taiwan News*, 22 September 2015, http://www.taiwannews.com.tw/etn/news_content.php?id=2808338 (accessed on 10 March 2016).

10

Maritime Security and the Indo-Pacific Security Link: The Strategic Reorientation of India and Taiwan

Fu-Kuo Liu

The concept of Indo-Pacific is to create a new 'strategic system' connecting the Indian Ocean and the Pacific Ocean.[1] Over the years, although there have been different interpretations of the concept by regional countries – Australia, Japan, the United States, India, and Indonesia – the main themes refer to economics, geopolitics and security. In addition, they could refer to the increasing importance of particular countries, notably the rise of China and India. This geographic combination signifies the important links of energy security and maritime security with regional security. As the major economies in East Asia heavily depend on crude oil, natural gas and raw materials shipped from the Middle East and Africa, the sea lines of communication (SLOCs) from the Indian Ocean to the Pacific Ocean have become critical to the strategic environment.

The current global power shift from West to East has confirmed the importance of East Asian dynamism to the world and further facilitated the critical connection of the two oceans. Since the turn of the century, this alarming tone has prevailed in most parts of the West.[2] As the East, mainly referring to the rise of the East Asian countries including China, increases its significance in the global economic, political and geostrategic affairs, its dependence on energy supply from the Middle East and Africa is growing to an unprecedented level. Energy supply routes from the Indian Ocean to the Pacific Ocean have become lifelines for many and have resulted in the shift of the strategic landscape. Two broader implications should also be taken into account. First, Indo-Pacific refers to the expansion of the geostrategic environment. In the perspective of maritime security, the common stake in protecting SLOCs throughout the region becomes salient to every state. Secondly, Indo-Pacific is originally driven by economic transactions and trading flows within the geographic context. East Asian countries rely more and more on the Indian Ocean for seaborne energy supply as well as for trade.

This chapter examines the significance of Indo-Pacific to the changing strategic environment in the region and the relevance of maritime security and energy security. Under the Indo-Pacific strategic context, it argues that geopolitical and geo-economic interest would drive a new ground of common interest for India and Taiwan. As such, it is time that India and Taiwan seek to reorient their strategy for further cooperation beyond non-political affairs.

Change of Strategic Environment and the Emergence of Indo-Pacific

The emergence of the Indo-Pacific concept implies a significant change of geopolitical and economic reality. Of course, China and India as important trading and strategic powers have brought about a change of geopolitical landscape in Asia.[3] As the East Asian economies grow fast, their dependence upon energy supply from the Middle East and Africa become critical for their sustained development. The East Asian economies also export industrial products to South Asia, Africa, the Middle East, and Europe through the Indian Ocean. As a result, increasing common stake has made the concept of Indo-Pacific more lively and convincing to the parties concerned. The concept has been officially emphasised by the different governments in the region, such as Australia, India, Japan, the United States, Indonesia, and Singapore.

The concept of Indo-Pacific mainly refers to the themes of economics, geopolitics and security and reflects recognising the new reality of growing connectivity between the Pacific Ocean and Indian Ocean. More significantly, this connectivity is creating a single 'strategic system'.[4] Because the emergence of new economies in the broader region becomes the centre of the global engine of economic development, it has shifted the focus of the power base and original geopolitical structure. As a result, it implies more for regional security and readjustment of the power restructure mainly referring to the four key powers: China, the United States, India, and Japan. Among others, Australia and Indonesia due to their geographic location first envisioned the relevance and strategic significance of Indo-Pacific. While observing the increasing economic and strategic weight of rising China, India and East Asia, the *2013 Australian Defence White Paper* emphasised the concept of Indo-Pacific as having great strategic significance and described its 'emergence as "a single strategic arc"'.[5] The *2016 Australian Defence White Paper* goes even further in emphasising the critical importance of Indo-Pacific.

A common feature of the economies involved in Indo-Pacific is their heavy reliance on seaborne energy imports. This makes maritime security critically important to the foundation of Indo-Pacific. The substance of maritime security in the Indo-Pacific context includes energy supply routes, transportation safety, assurance of maritime security, and geopolitical rebalance.

Maritime Security and Strategic Significance of Indo-Pacific

As a single strategic system is increasingly formed through economic transactions, energy supply, diplomatic manipulation, and big power strategic competition, maritime security is at the core of Indo-Pacific. Although many in East Asia emphasise the economic significance of Indo-Pacific, they do recognise its broader strategic significance. China and India have, in particular, generated major momentum for the emergence of Indo-Pacific. When China steps up its overall efforts in the maritime domain including trade, energy, transportation and strategic advance, its vision on maritime strategy has been a focal point of observation.

China is rapidly increasing its dependency upon oil from the Middle

East and Africa. Roughly 85 per cent of all oil imported by China passes through the Strait of Malacca.[6] As an energy-scarce state, China is increasingly dependent on maritime shipment through Indo-Pacific. To protect its energy supply, trade and national interest, China is driven to step up its military presence and power projection in the Indian Ocean. China may for now have doubts about the emergence of the Indo-Pacific strategic system, while India, Australia, the United States and Japan have publicly advocated its implication for strategic advance to deter China's expansionism. Although the Chinese government has not yet responded formally to the idea of Indo-Pacific, its latest grand strategy, the 21st Century Maritime Silk Road, reflects the Indo-Pacific context.

In a similar vein, India under Prime Minister Narendra Modi chants for its Act East policy, and US President Barack Obama continues to push through his country's Rebalance to Asia strategy. China's Maritime Silk Road, India's Act East policy and US Rebalance to Asia are part of the big-power competition for influence in Indo-Pacific.

In March 2015, the US Navy released its document, 'A Cooperative Strategy for 21st Century Sea Power', which emphasised the strategic idea of Indo-Asia-Pacific. This implies that the US military calculates the importance of a strategic shift and endorses the concept and increasing significance of Indo-Pacific. The US has recognised that 'the economic importance, security interests, and geography of this vast maritime region dictate a growing reliance on naval forces to protect US interests and maintain an enduring commitment to the stability of the region.'[7] Increasing dependence upon the transportation routes of the Indian Ocean indicates that the security stakes are rising.

According to its proclaimed strategy, the US will by 2020 shift 60 per cent of its naval forces into the region to cope with new challenges to its national interest. The US will not only enhance its war-fighting advantages in the theatre through 'improved interoperability, more integrated operations, and increasingly complex exercises and training', but also enhance partnerships with regional players through 'expanded maritime security operations, shared maritime domain awareness, and longer multilateral engagements.'[8] As such, the US Navy and Marine Corps have strengthened their forward deployment in the Indo-Pacific region. The

Marine Corps' deployment to Darwin, Australia, reflects the United States' strategic consideration in Indo-Pacific and is very much aligned with the Indo-Pacific 'strategic arc'.

When China's and India's economic development accelerates further, increase in their energy demand would definitely heighten their dependence on maritime security for energy supply and trade flows. The countries concerned in the region, i.e. the US, India, Australia, Indonesia, Japan, and China will all respond to the strategic importance of Indo-Pacific. It is almost inevitable that all related countries will try to strengthen their naval control and alliance for assurance of the sea lanes from the Indian Ocean through the Pacific Ocean. Today, in the context of Indo-Pacific, the region is witnessing three kinds of developments: first, booming trade flows and increasing energy demands identify the critical importance of the region; second, China's naval forces are trying to stretch its reach into the Indian Ocean to protect its increasing interests in maritime involvement and gain access to supply markets of energy resources; third, by deploying naval forces in the Indian Ocean, China would lift its weight in the competing share of strategic room against Indian and US interests.

India-Taiwan Strategic Reorientation

Strategically, India depends more on sea trade than land routes. India's northern front has a complicated geography discouraging trade. The Indian Ocean provides convenient accesses for trade, transportation of energy and communication. As India is rising, its economic development, commercial growth, political stability and national security are all dependent on the security of sea lanes and maritime security surrounding India. According to an IMF projection, India will economically grow faster than China in 2015-2016. The recent Russian energy strategy is to diversify its dependence on European markets and broaden its export to China and India. Especially, Russia is concerned that China's economy is slowing down in 2015 and beyond and has taken a more proactive marketing strategy to get access to the Indian market. During the India-Russia Summit in December 2014, President Putin and Prime Minister Modi signed several critical agreements to facilitate bilateral cooperation, particularly on energy, involving oil and gas.[9] On the maritime front, India will increasingly depend on maritime imports from Russia's Far East.[10]

As India is looking more to the East in terms of its Act East policy for economic and security cooperation, it has widened its security stake with regional countries, especially in terms of sharing maritime interest. Around 55 per cent of India's trade in Asia-Pacific transits through the South China Sea region. India's trade and energy supply policies have increased the importance of Indo-Pacific as a single strategic system.

There are two key points regarding India's orientation in Indo-Pacific. First, its growing energy demand has made India connect with Asia-Pacific more comprehensively in order to ensure the region's maritime security. The International Energy Agency's *World Economic Outlook 2015* projects that India will have the fastest growth in energy demand from 2014 to 2040, in contrast to China's slowing energy demand.[11] In 2015, India has also overtaken China as the global number one importer of coal.[12] When India relies even more on energy imports in the years ahead, freedom of navigation in Indo-Pacific will have to be assured. The Indian Navy will increase its presence in Indo-Pacific, especially in the Asia-Pacific region, as India's new maritime strategy sets the Indian Ocean out to be a foreign policy priority. India's objective is also to maintain maritime dominance to counter China's expansionism in the Indian Ocean.[13] In this regard, the South China Sea becomes a critical strategic pivot for India.

Secondly, India's Act East policy has rolled into South-East Asia and East Asia. On the level of multilateral cooperation mechanisms, the Indian perspective of Indo-Pacific focuses more on ASEAN-centred mechanisms for regional cooperation, e.g. ASEAN-plus, East Asian Summit (EAS), ASEAN Defence Ministerial Meetings plus (ADMM+) than traditional Asia Pacific-centred regionalism, i.e. Asia-Pacific Economic Conference (APEC). Through these regional multilateral mechanisms, India would find it easier to broaden its connection with regional countries in its neighbourhood and Asia-Pacific. As such, India's interest will be attached to the dynamism of East Asian economic development. Beyond economic cooperation, regional security cooperation also greatly concerns India's interest. China's rise has changed the strategic landscape in Asia.

How does Taiwan respond to the Indo-Pacific link and India's Act East policy? Has it developed a new strategy to accommodate the strategic change in the larger regional context? So far, Taiwan is very much stuck in domestic political tangles and the cross-Taiwan Strait relation, as the outgoing KMT government has become politically weak and the incoming government is still trying to figure out a probable common ground with Beijing. Before it can solve the difficulties and differences with Beijing, there would hardly be any elaboration going beyond the Taiwan Strait.

In practice, however, the way Taiwan has been conducting external trade, energy supply, shipping through the Indian Ocean and the Pacific Ocean is all very much along the line of the Indo-Pacific concept. Although Taiwan is not a significant political player in the region, it does take a unique geopolitical perspective in responding to the importance of Indo-Pacific.

For up to 98.04 per cent of its energy requirements Taiwan relies on imports. In 2014 Taiwan's overall energy reliance was on oil (48.52 per cent), natural gas (12.23 per cent), coal (29.20 per cent), nuclear energy (8.33 per cent), hydropower (0.49 per cent) and others (1.23 per cent).[14] Major energy imports (oil and gas) are from the Middle East and Africa. Taiwan's pattern of energy supply is very similar to that of Japan and South Korea. Its oil suppliers accounted for 81.6 per cent from the Middle East. Taiwan therefore is very vulnerable to any strategic change in maritime energy supply routes. Its unique political status and weak political posture in the international community has made it further vulnerable in this regard.

Taiwan's overall pattern of external trade and energy supply reflects its clear orientation to Indo-Pacific. Due to the political difficulty in establishing official links with other governments and intergovernmental organisations, Taiwan does not have diplomatic and political relationship with countries along the SLOCs. In view of the strategic shift and the emergence of Indo-Pacific, Taiwan will support the idea of securing SLOCs and freedom of navigation.

Over the last 20 years after they redeveloped quasi-diplomatic links, India and Taipei mostly worked on the official domains of economic, trade, technological, cultural, and educational cooperation. Due to political concerns about diplomatic pressure from China, India has kept a low profile while maintaining substantial contacts with Taiwan, while leaving the strategic areas untouched. As the mutual strategic interest generated by the emergence of Indo-Pacific increases, there is a growing need to review and reorient strategic planning of traditional wisdom on both sides. India is developing its Act East policy as a way of competing with the fast expanding China. Indo-Pacific may also imply more chances for cooperation and competition between China and India.

In the Indo-Pacific geopolitical context, Taiwan's strategic location and sharing strategic interest with India would strengthen the route of common interest between the two sides. Currently, Taiwan's involvement in maritime territorial claims in the East China Sea and South China Sea makes it a critical player in regional maritime territorial disputes. For strengthening its national security and for protecting its maritime interest and sovereignty, Taiwan is stepping up its military presence and diplomatic effort. Taiwan's dependence upon the Indian Ocean and SLOCs through the South China Sea will increase further, as strategic interest will be added to the present basis of economic transaction and energy supply. India will also enhance its maritime strategy in guarding against any potential interruption of communication in the sea. For both India and Taiwan, maritime security and energy security will be critical areas of cooperation.

Concluding Remarks

A strategic shift has taken shape in terms of the Indo-Pacific concept, driving the countries involved to respond positively. The region has witnessed US rebalance to Asia extending to the Indian Ocean, India's Act East policy materialising its accession to Asia-Pacific, and China's Maritime Silk Road connecting the Pacific and Indian Ocean. In this context, Indo-Pacific will become a ground of strategic competition for the big powers. The US, India, Japan, and Australia are currently referring to the geopolitical significance of Indo-Pacific as a counter to China's continuous expansion.

In the larger geopolitical context, India and Taiwan may have to add some new policy ingredients in their bilateral relations. Beyond cooperation in economic, cultural and technological affairs, a strategic partnership to strengthen the Indian presence in Asia-Pacific and to secure Taiwan's seaborne trade and energy transportation in the Indian Ocean would be regarded as responding to the emergence of Indo-Pacific in today's geopolitical transformation.

NOTES

1. 'Redefining the region: the Indo-Pacific idea', *Asia-Pacific Regional Security Assessment 2015: Key Developments and Trends* (London: International Institute for Strategic Studies, 2015), p. 9.
2. Michael Cox, 'Power shifts, economic change and the decline of the west?' Foreign and Commonwealth Office, UK Government, 28 November 2012, https://www.gov.uk/government/publications/power-shifts-economic-change-and-the-decline-of-the-west/
3. *Asia-Pacific Regional Security Assessment 2015: Key Developments and Trends* (London: International Institute for Strategic Studies, 2015), pp. 7-9.
4. Ibid.
5. *Defence White Paper 2013*, Department of Defence, Australian Government. http://www.defence.gov.au/whitepaper/2013/docs/wp_2013_web.pdf
6. 'China is hooked on Mideast oil, which helps build a good case for a Petroyaun', FAILAKA, 24 January 2014, http://failaka.com/china-is-hooked-on-mideast-oil/
7. 'A cooperative strategy for 21st century sea power', US Navy, March 2015, p. 3, http://www.navy.mil/local/maritime/150227-CS21R-Final.pdf
8. Ibid., p. 14.
9. Gaurav Agnihotri, 'With China Slowdown, Russia Looks to India', Oilprice.com, 10 September 2015, http://oilprice.com/Energy/Energy-General/With-China-Slowdown-Russia-Looks-To-India.html
10. 'BPCL buys first shipment of Russian Far East crude grade', *Business News*, 29 July 2015, http://in.reuters.com/article/2015/07/29/india-crude-idINKCN0Q30MU20150729
11. Ragini Bhuyan, 'Five charts that show how India's dependence on fossil fuels will increase', Live Mint, 13 November 2015, http://www.livemint.com/Opinion/Lc6lOXOiSwzSWPWF1yTvTI/Five-charts-that-show-how-Indias-dependence-on-fossil-fuels.html
12. Benny Peiser, 'India to Overtake China as the World's Biggest Coal Importer', Climate Change Dispatch, 17 April 2015, http://www.climatechangedispatch.com/india-to-overtake-china-as-the-world-s-biggest-coal-importer.html
13. 'India's new maritime strategy', *IISS Strategic Comments*, Volume 2015, Edition number: 37 (01 December 2015).
14. *Energy Statistics Hand Book 2014,* Bureau of Energy, Ministry of Economic Affairs, ROC, 2015, http://web3.moeaboe.gov.tw/ECW/english/content/SubMenu.aspx?menu_id=1537

11

India and Taiwan: Partnering in Cyber Security

Cherian Samuel

Cyber security has become a critical component of national security in recent years. Networks have become integral to the economic, political, financial and social fabric of both developed and emerging countries. However, efforts to secure this crucial resource at the global level are still fragmented and rudimentary. The same holds true even for bilateral cooperation for a variety of reasons. As titans in hardware and software, Taiwan and India, respectively, have sufficient reason to cooperate in cyberspace issues. However, the two governments are yet to take the lead in providing direction and impetus for cooperation. This is despite the fact that they both are victims to cyber attacks from the same source(s), and can benefit immensely from sharing information and resources to combat the cyber threat.

India in Cyberspace: A Snapshot

India today has the second-largest internet user base in the world after China. The approximately 314 million Indians online make up about 28 per cent of the 1.2 billion population. However, the sheer numbers, even with such low internet penetration, pose challenges to not just companies, but also the government and agencies responsible for ensuring the safety and security of cyberspace.

Many commentaries refer to India as a cyber power, something that might appear to beat odds with the frequent reports regarding the vulnerabilities in India's cyber security. Though India was one of the earlier countries to promulgate an Information Technology Bill and set up a Computer Emergency Responses Team (CERT), subsequently it began to lag behind in enhancing cyber security. Over the years, there have been large-scale intrusions by malicious actors into sensitive networks and breaches of critical information infrastructure. According to a statement made by the Minister of Communication in Parliament in December 2015, a total number of 22,060, 71,780, 130,338, and 49,504 cyber-security incidents including phishing, scanning, spam, malicious code, website intrusion, etc. were reported during the years 2012, 2013 and 2014, respectively. The Minister further said that a total of 27,605, 28,481 and 32,323 websites were hacked by various hacker groups during the same period.[1] A majority of these attacks were traced to IP addresses in a few countries, including Pakistan and China. This has been corroborated by a number of reports over the years from cyber security companies.

Even though it was the 2008 Mumbai terrorist attack that led to the enactment of the IT Amendment Act with focus on cyber security, there is a lack of both capabilities and capacities to counter cyber threats. A National Cyber Security Policy (NCSP) was announced in 2013 with the objectives of (1) creating a secure cyberspace ecosystem and (2) strengthening the regulatory framework. The architecture to implement the policy is only gradually being put in place. Among the proposed initiatives intended to build capacity in cyber security are a national Cyber Security Coordination Centre, an e-Governance Security Centre, initiatives to encourage manufacturing of electronic products within the country, and a Centre of Excellence in the 'Internet of things'. A National Cyber Security Coordinator has been appointed to coordinate cyber security activities. All this activity on the part of the government has also enthused the private sector, which despite owning much of the infrastructure of cyberspace, has so far shied away from taking responsibility for its security, arguing that providing security, physical or virtual, is the responsibility of the government. That harkens back to the development of ICT in Asia where the primary agent in developing the ICT sector was the government even in then advanced Asian countries such as Japan, South Korea and Malaysia.

Recent Initiatives

Cyber security has become even more crucial to the country's security following the announcement of programmes like Digital India, which seeks to deliver all manner of services to the citizen through digital means. Digital India seeks to provide an overall framework and leverage the use of IT to better serve the citizens. In a recent speech at NASSCOM, the Prime Minister said that his vision is 'a Digital India where government services are easily and efficiently available on mobile devices; where government actively engages with people on social media; where mobile phones enable personal services; and where cyber security becomes an integral part of the national security.'[2]

Digital India has nine so-called pillars, which broadly seek to provide digital infrastructure as a utility to every citizen, governance and services on demand, and digital empowerment. The cumulative expenditure on Digital India would be in the region of a billion dollars. There are other programmes related to financial inclusion that are closely tied in with this programme. For instance, the number of debit cards issued has gone up by 100 million as part of the programme to create bank accounts in rural areas. This capacity building for the citizens also has enormous implications for security, and specifically cyber security. As more people get exposed to technology when they avail government services online, conduct financial transactions through mobiles, or simply surf the internet using Wi-Fi at colleges, the risks will also go up manifold. Therefore, as Digital India scales up and cyber enables millions of people, both the core infrastructure and the individuals at the edges become targets of a variety of actors, from state-sponsored proxy actors, to international crime syndicates. In addition to this, there are any number of other issues directly related to cyber security, such as data protection, to supply chain integrity, and indirect issues such as internet governance that can also affect the security of a state. Many of these issues were raised in the National Cyber Security Policy. For instance, Section H of the NCSP on the 'Promotion of Research & Development in Cyber Security' called for encouragement of 'Research & Development to produce cost-effective, tailor-made, indigenous security solutions meeting a wide range of cyber security challenges and target for export markets.' Some of these concerns are addressed through the Make in India programme, which encourages foreign companies to manufacture products in India. A more recent initiative, launched in January 2016, is the Startup India campaign, aimed at providing enablers for start-ups to succeed. The campaign is similar to the Headstart Taiwan project started by the Taiwan National Development Council in 2015, which also seeks to improve the environment for nascent entrepreneurs and reduce paperwork and red tape that usually accompanies setting up companies. A fourth initiative that ties in with the previous campaigns is the Skill India initiative, which seeks to skill and up-skill 400 million people by 2022.[3]

At the international level, India has been proactive in various multilateral fora from the United Nations to the International Telecommunication Union (ITU). It was a member of several Groups of Governmental Experts (GGE) on cyber security and has strongly supported confidence-building measures in cyberspace. India has also been active at the various meetings of the ITU. In the last plenipotentiary meeting at Busan in 2014, India put forward a proposal on ITU's Role in Realizing Secure Information Society (Proposal 98).[4] This called for a 'traffic routing plan' to 'effectively ensure the traceability of communication', citing cyber security concerns arising out of the fact that there was no way to trace the origin of malicious data and traffic.

India has also embraced multi-stakeholder internet governance, as per the Tunis Agenda which defined Internet Governance as 'the development and application by governments, the private sector and civil society, in their respective roles, of shared principles, norms, rules, decision-making procedures, and programmes that shape the evolution and use of the Internet.'

At the bilateral level, cyber security dialogues have been initiated with various countries including Japan, South Korea, the United Kingdom,

France, the United States, the European Union, Malaysia and Singapore, covering various facets of cyber security.

Scope for Cooperation

There is tremendous scope for cooperation between India and Taiwan in the cyber security space. Both countries have natural interests and complementarities. While India is an IT and software superpower with exports touching (US)$100 billion, more than 40 per cent of Taiwan's total exports are made up of electronic components. However, most of this goes to China and is in turn exported as finished electronics products to various countries. Consequently, while electronics imports from China to India were in the range of $18.5 billion in 2015, electronics imports from Taiwan amounted to $525 million, about half a per cent of Taiwan's total electronic exports of $125 billion. With the thrust provided to manufacturing under Make in India, there is a case to be made for some of the electronic manufacturing undertaken by Taiwan to be shifted to India.

There has been interest in manufacturing in India on the part of Taiwanese companies. Foxconn has announced it is investing up to US$20 billion to set up plants and an entire manufacturing ecosystem over the coming years.[5] This investment makes both strategic and economic sense as there are increasing concerns over backdoors in hardware products. This would take care of the many concerns in India about the integrity and potential for mischief inherent in such large-scale imports of electronics items from China. Other companies such as Acer, HTC and Asus are also looking to increase investment and market share in India.

On the cyber security front, Taiwan has been subject to large-scale cyber attacks similar to those faced by India, and for much longer. These is much scope for sharing of information and best practices since Taiwan has gone much further than India in building up a defensive capability and has intimate knowledge of the attackers and types of attacks. While Taiwan is inhibited by the fact that it is excluded from groupings such as the UN GGE, it is a member of APCERT, joining in 2003. It is also a part of the APEC cyber-related working groups. However, it is excluded from the ASEAN and ASEAN Regional Forum working groups.[6] Given that cyber security is a global concern, mechanisms such as APCERT in which both countries are members should be strengthened and become an effective forum for resolving cyber security issues.

On the governmental side, there is scope for closer cooperation and exchange of information on cyber attacks and cyber security incident management and best practices, but ultimately, it is synergies in the commercial space that will lubricate such exchanges. This is where developments like Foxconn's investment will make a difference and provide the much-needed push factor to cyber security cooperation. On the economic side, governments have a role to play in responding to constraints such as cultural disparities, ease of doing business, improving connectivity, and creating awareness about the opportunities available.

Conclusion

For India, the internal challenges, in a nutshell, include building up capacities at home to provide a safe and secure cyberspace, particularly with regard to law enforcement, judicial, forensic capabilities; continuous updation of national cyber security policies to deal with new challenges from cloud computing to the internet of things; and better implementation of rules and regulations. Better interface between the public sector and private sector, creating opportunities for manufacturing within the country, cultivating a start-up culture to propel innovation and enhancing cooperation between academia, industry and the government are the other challenges before the government. All these are similar to the challenges faced by the Taiwan government and offer opportunities to exchange best practices.

Ultimately, in the Asian context, national governments still play a crucial role in deciding the flow of technologies, human resources and capital, and provide the necessary push through policies for the private sector to follow through. Given that there are undeniable strategic benefits to cooperating on issues related to cyber security, as well as economic spinoffs, both governments should make a determined effort to identify and remove the obstacles that are preventing cooperation from achieving the necessary momentum to get off the ground.

Given the wealth of knowledge and experience on cyber threats that resides in Taiwan, there is a case to be made for increased cooperation on cyber security with Taiwan. This could be formalised through MoUs between respective technical bodies in the two countries facilitating the exchange of best practices and information related to various types of attacks. In doing so, the pitfalls that are inherent to such cooperation should be avoided. In the first instance, the two countries have different levels of expertise and the responsibility for cyber security is vested in different authorities. Secondly, much of the infrastructure and expertise is in the private sector in both countries. Thirdly, given the sensitivity of networks, there is a disinclination to share the vulnerabilities that exist. Even very close allies such as the United States and Japan have found it difficult to sustain cyber security cooperation. Therefore, very precise parameters have to be drawn for cyber security cooperation to succeed.[7]

NOTES

1. *India Today*, 'Government says most cyber attacks on India are from Pakistan, China', 7 August 2015, http://indiatoday.intoday.in/technology/story/government-says-most-cyberattacks-on-india-are-from-pakistan-china/1/457046.html
2. *Daily News Analysis*, Digital India highlights… 2 July 2015, http://www.firstpost.com/business/digital-india-highlights-rs-4-5-lakh-cr-investment-in-governance-18-lakh-jobs-and-i-dream-of-2321734.html
3. *Economic Times*, Government to train 40 crore people under Skill India initiative, 21 July 2015, http://economictimes.indiatimes.com/articleshow/48090083.cms
4. http://www.itu.int/md/S14-PP-C-0098/en
5. *Economic Times*, Foxconn boost for 'Make in India': Why Taiwan's growing interests in India deserve attention, 16 August 2015, http://telecom.economictimes.indiatimes.com/news/industry/foxconn-boost-for-make-in-india-why-taiwans-growing-interests-in-india-deserve-attention/48499061
6. Bonnie S. Glaser and Jacqueline A. Vitello, *Taiwan's Marginalized Role in International Security: Paying a Price,* CSIS/Rowman & Littlefield, 2015, https://csis.org/files/publication/150105_Glaser_TaiwanMarginalizedRole_WEB.pdf

Index